英語でホッカイドー
PERA PERAトーク 500

遠藤昌子
ENDO Masako

北海道新聞社

Prologue
はじめに

　2008年に前作の『PERAPERAホッカイドー　英語で北海道をガイドする本』を北海道新聞社から出版しました。本は「わかりやすくて、覚えやすい！」と、中学、高校、大学、通訳養成学校などでテキストに使っていただきました。学生だけでなく、プロの通訳ガイド、ホテルのコンシェルジュ、旅行会社社員、タクシードライバーなどの方々も、「仕事に役立つ」と愛用してくださいました。

　道庁経済部の統計によれば、当時北海道を訪問する外国人は年間約68万人でした。その後、東日本大震災で一時落ち込んだものの、2013年度には約115万人に達しました。東南アジア諸国からの日本入国ビザの発給が要件緩和されたのに加え、直行便の就航、リピーターの個人客が大幅に増えたことも大きな要因です。

　外国人の来道者数が増えると、ホテルやバスなどに加えて、外国語を話すガイドがより多く必要になります。北海道に来る外国人の多くは英語を話すため、北海道地域限定通訳案内士（現在は休止）、札幌市特区通訳案内士などが育成されてきました。全道にある多くの語学ボランティア団体も研鑽を重ねています。

　じつは、英語でコミュニケーションできる人を増やすことは、北海道を訪問する外国人を増やすためのカギになります。地元の人との触れ合いや会話が、北海道旅行の満足感をグーンと高めるからです。

　では、かれらは北海道観光に何を求めているのでしょうか。私がこれまで出会った多くの外国人は、北海道人（道産子）の暮らしぶりを知りたがりました。
「雪かきはだれかを雇うの？」（夫の無償の愛！）

「庭の木は冬に枯れるの？」（枯れませんってば！）
「部屋は寒くないの？」（Tシャツでビール！）
「トイレは洗浄機能付き？」（たいていの家で！）
「毎日カニを食べるの？」（とんでもない！）
「あなたもスキージャンプするの？」（まさかっ！）
　……などなど。

　北海道の歴史や文化にも興味津々です。マリモやタンチョウに感動し、エゾシカの親子に歓声をあげ、流氷や摩周湖を神秘的と言いました。今回の本は、そんな魅力いっぱいの北海道と道産子の暮らしを英語で伝えるための本です。

　グリーンシーズンに訪れた人々は、色彩豊かで雄大な景色、個性的な温泉、おいしい食事を堪能し、「北海道大好き！」とリピーターになりました。さらに近年は、ホワイトシーズンの訪問者が増えています。雪や氷のフェスティバル、夜空に映えるイルミネーション、新雪を滑走する豪快なスノーモービル、カラフルなテントでの氷上ワカサギ釣り……。寒くて長い冬が、魅力的な季節に変身したのです。

　今や北海道は、四季を通して外国人憧れの人気スポットになりました。東京オリンピックが開かれる2020年には外国人観光客がさらに増えると言われています。あなたが外国人に英語でホッカイドーを伝えるチャンスは明日かもしれません！

　付録のCDには、前作に続きアマンダ・ハーロウさんの美しい英国風英語で基本例文がすべて収録されています。一緒に声を出して、何度も繰り返し発声練習をしてみてください。きっと自然に英語が口をついて出てきますよ！

絵一語でGO!

⑧ 富良野市 / メロン食べ放題に挑戦、食べすぎてお腹をこわす。
Furano: I tried all-you-can-eat melon. I ate too much and had diarrhea.

⑨ 層雲峡 / 石狩河岸で野宿。星がきれいだ!
Sounkyo Gorge: I slept outdoors on the banks of on the Ishikari River. I saw thousands of twinkling stars!

⑩ 大雪山 / 旭岳で野天風呂に入る。蚊に刺されるが肌はピカピカ。痒い……
Mt Taisetsu Range: I took a dip in an open air bath on Mt. Asahi. The bath made my skin smoother, but bitten by lots of mosquitoes……itchy.

⑪ 旭川 / レッサーパンダとにらめっこ。
Asahikawa: I got into a staring match with a red panda.

⑫ 札幌 / 羊ヶ丘でヒツジに追いかけられる。冗談みたいだけどホントの話。
Sapporo: On Hitsujigaoka (sheep Hill), some sheep started chasing me. No kidding. It's true.

⑬ 小樽 / オルゴールを壊してしまい弁償するトホホ
Otaru: I broke a music box and I had to pay for it. Great….

⑭ ニセコ / 羊蹄山のてっぺんからオカンに愛を叫ぶ(ボクはマザコンだったんだ?)
Niseko: From the top Mt. Yotei. I shouted my love to my mom. (Am I a momma's boy after all?)

⑮ 函館 / ヤリイカを釣る。
Hakodate: I fished for spear squid.

⑯ 南茅部 / 縄文土偶から愛を告白される!ボク?
Minamikayabe: A clay Jomon figurine confessed her love to me. Me?

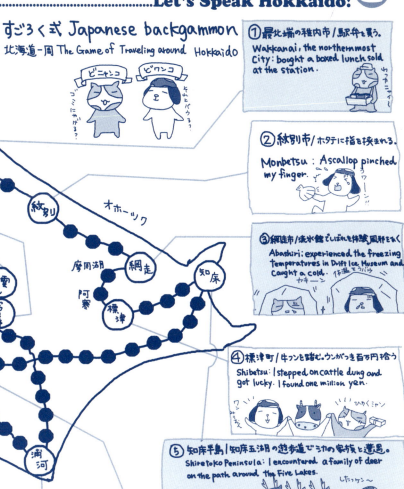

絵一語でGO!

仲良くしてね

―基本形① ○○は、○○です(ます)。―

My sister is 【naturally a bit spacy】
お姉ちゃんは天然です。

Dosanko, the Hokkaido locals are 【open minded】
どさんこはあけっぴろげ（気さく）です。

Jealous of
妬みっぽい

not honest
うそつき

naturally a bit spacy
天然ボケ

a two timer
二股で恋愛

easy going
のんき

stubborn
頑固者

optimistic
楽天家

a big spender
浪費家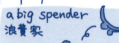

talkative
おしゃべり

My cat is 【jealous of】my new girlfriend.
猫ちゃんがオレの新しい彼女に妬いているよ。

My friend Kyunchan is 【shy】
ともだちのキュンちゃんははずかしがりやさん。

Terebitosan is 【devoted to his family】
テレビ父さんは家族思いですから〜

My ex-boyfriend was 【a two timer】
モトカレったら二股かけていたんだよ。

Let's Speak Hokkaido! ②

my sister 姉

my brother 弟

my cousin いとこ

my ex-boyfriend モトカレ

my ex-ex-girlfriend モトのモトカノ

my boss 上司

my dentist いきつけの歯医者

my turtle ペットの亀

an alien 宇宙人

my neighbor Totoro ヒなりのトトロ

my friend Kyunchan 友達のキュンちゃん

Terebitosan, テレビ父さん

基本形② ○○は、○○に夢中です。

My best friend is into 【Mr. Otani, a baseball player】
親友は大谷君の追っかけに夢中です。

My sister is into 【husband hunting】
姉は婚活中。

---

cosplay コスプレ

visiting roadside stations 道の駅

growing vegetables in the backyard 家庭菜園

husband (wife) hunting 婚活

preparation for living your last days happily 終活

dinosaur movies 恐竜映画

Hatsune Miku 初音ミク

snow shoveling 雪かき

salmon fishing 鮭釣り

すし屋に行ったら　At a sushi restaurant

How many of you are there?
何人ですか？

Do you use chopsticks?
箸を使いますか？

It's OK to eat sushi with your fingers.
手で食べてもかまいません。

Would you like to have some soup?
汁ものはいりますか？

Cucumber rolls are good.
キュウリ巻がおすすめです。
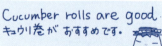

Do you want to try a natto roll?
納豆巻に挑戦してみますか？

Would you like to have more wasabi?
わさび、もっともらいましょうか？

Let's Speak Hokkaido! ③

It's delicious!
おいしいです。

I don't like it so much.
あまり好きではありません。

I don't like fish eggs.
魚卵は苦手です。

What is this?
これは何ですか？

Do you want to have the sashimi grilled?
ネタをあぶってもらいますか？

This fish is very fresh!
この魚は新鮮ですね！

Check please.
お勘定をお願いします。

Let me pay today.
今日は私がおごります。

You can pay the next time.
次回はおごってくださいね。

Let's split the bill.
割り勘にしましょう。

Do you take credit cards?
カードで支払いはできますか？

I need a receipt.
領収書をください。

Let's Speak Hokkaido!

Contents
目次

Prologue はじめに ………………………………… 002
絵一語で GO！………………………………………… 004

Part 1　Welcome to Hokkaido!
ようこそ

❶ 出会い ………………………………………………… 016
❷ 交通 …………………………………………………… 018
❸ 住宅事情 ……………………………………………… 020
❹ 言葉 …………………………………………………… 022
❺ 血液型占い …………………………………………… 024
❻ 予定 …………………………………………………… 026
❼ 神社 …………………………………………………… 028
❽ コンビニ ……………………………………………… 030
❾ 病気 …………………………………………………… 032
❿ 学校 …………………………………………………… 034
⓫ 仕事 …………………………………………………… 036
⓬ 北海道の食 …………………………………………… 038
⓭ 食事 …………………………………………………… 040
⓮ そば打ち ……………………………………………… 042
⓯ 別れ …………………………………………………… 044

Part 2 Enjoy Hokkaido Life!
季節を感じて

- ⑯ 春が来た ……………………… 048
- ⑰ 桜 ……………………………… 050
- ⑱ 夏の楽しみ …………………… 052
- ⑲ お盆 …………………………… 054
- ⑳ 食欲の秋 ……………………… 056
- ㉑ 晩秋 …………………………… 058
- ㉒ 冬の始まり …………………… 060
- ㉓ 雪 ……………………………… 062
- ㉔ 大晦日 ………………………… 064
- ㉕ お正月 ………………………… 066
- ㉖ 雪仕事 ………………………… 068
- ㉗ 冬祭り ………………………… 070
- ㉘ 春を待つ ……………………… 072
- ㉙ セグウェイ …………………… 074
- ㉚ 野球観戦 ……………………… 076
- ㉛ アイスクリーム作り ………… 078
- ㉜ 果物狩り ……………………… 080
- ㉝ スキー場 ……………………… 082
- ㉞ スノーモービル ……………… 084
- ㉟ ワカサギ釣り ………………… 086

Part 3　Discover Hokkaido!
ザ・北海道

- ㊱ クラーク博士 …… 090
- ㊲ 三松正夫と有珠山 …… 092
- ㊳ 竹鶴とリタ …… 094
- ㊴ マリモ …… 096
- ㊵ 流氷 …… 098
- ㊶ タンチョウ …… 100
- ㊷ エゾシカ …… 102
- ㊸ 利尻と礼文 …… 104
- ㊹ 摩周湖 …… 106
- ㊺ 小樽運河 …… 108
- ㊻ 札幌オリンピック …… 110
- ㊼ 青函トンネル …… 112
- ㊽ ワインとチーズ …… 114
- ㊾ サケ …… 116

知ってるつもり?!　アジア編1 …… 046
　　　　　　　　　アジア編2 …… 088
　　　　　　　　　イスラム編 …… 118

［資料編］知っておきたい！ ガイドの基本ABC …… 119

Part 1

Welcome to Hokkaido!
[ようこそ]

外国の人たちは北海道の何が好き？特にアジアの人々に人気のHokkaidoベスト10をご紹介します。

アジア人に人気の 北海道グルメベスト10
①すし ②刺し身 ③カニ ④海鮮丼 ⑤ラーメン ⑥アイスクリーム
⑦チーズケーキ ⑧海鮮バーベキュー ⑨そば ⑩海鮮懐石料理

Part1／Welcome to Hokkaido!

01 出会い / Hello!
ようこそ北海道へ！ / Welcome to Hokkaido!

CD-01

01 よろしくお願いします。遠藤理恵子です。

Nice to meet you. My name is Rieko Endo.

02 飛行機はいかがでしたか？

How was your flight?

03 時差ボケはしていませんか？

Do you have jet lag?

04 トイレに行きたいですか？

Do you need to use the restroom?

05 空港でお昼を食べていきましょうか？

Would you like to have lunch at the airport?

06 天気予報によると今日は曇りです。

The weather forecast says it will be cloudy today.

07 今日の札幌の最高気温は12度です。

Today's high in Sapporo will be 12 degrees Celsius.

08 北海道は初めてですか？

Is this your first visit to Hokkaido?

09 外は寒いのでジャケットを着てください。

You'll need to wear your jacket. It's cold outside.

10 荷物を持つのを手伝いましょうか？

Let me help you with your bags.

11 こちらです。私について来てください。

This way, please. Just follow me.

ようこそ 出会い

55語
ガイド

こんにちは！ ようこそ札幌にいらっしゃいました。私は仮屋です。カーリーと呼んでください。お目にかかれてうれしいです。飛行機では休めましたか？ トイレは大丈夫ですか？ そうですか、それではエレベーターで降りましょう。列車の駅までは歩いて3分です。札幌への列車は15分おきにあります。

Hi! Welcome to Sapporo! My name is Kariya. You can call me Curly! I am happy to meet you! Did you rest on the plane? Do you need to go to the restroom? OK. Let's take the elevator down. The train station is just a 3-minute walk from here. There is a train to Sapporo every 15 minutes.

| A | アジア各国でドラえもんが人気！
和室に通され、「のび太」をマネして
押し入れで寝てしまったマレーシア人がいたよ。 |

Part1／Welcome to Hokkaido!

02 交通 / Train and Bus
キタカを買いますか？
Do you want to buy Kitaka, a transport card?

CD-02

01 新千歳空港からは列車で札幌駅まで行きます。

We'll take the train from New Chitose Airport to Sapporo.

02 札幌駅からは地下鉄で澄川駅まで行きます。

From Sapporo Station, we'll take the subway to Sumikawa Station.

03 次に、澄川駅からバスで私の家に行きます。

Then from Sumikawa Station we'll catch a bus to my house.

04 地下鉄はグリーンラインなので覚えておいてください。

Remember this subway line is the Green Line.

05 この券売機は英語表示にもなります。

This ticket machine also shows fares in English.

06 優先席には高齢者や障害者、妊婦が座ります。

Priority seats are for the elderly, the handicapped, and expectant mothers.

07 車内では携帯電話での通話は禁止です。

Talking on the phone is not allowed on subway cars.

08 バス停はここです。時刻表を見ましょう。

This is our bus stop. Let's look at the time table.

09 ほら、25番のバスが来ました。乗りましょう。

Here comes the No. 25 bus. Let's get on.

10 整理券を取ってください。運賃は降りる時に払います。

Take a number ticket when you get on. We'll pay when we get off.

11 次に降りるのでブザーを押してください。

We'll get off at the next stop. Please push the button.

12 わが家はバス停から歩いて5分です。

My house is a 5-minute walk from the bus stop.

55語ガイド

1971年、札幌冬季オリンピック開催に備えて地下鉄が開通しました。ゴムタイヤを使っているので振動が少なく静かですよ。現在はグリーン、オレンジ、ブルーの3路線が運行されています。雪が降ると道路は渋滞することがあるのですが、地下鉄は常に時刻表のとおりです。

The Sapporo subway system started in 1971, one year before the Sapporo Winter Olympics. The trains run smoothly and with less noise because rubber tires are used. Now there are three lines: Orange, Green and Blue. The subway always runs on time, even in winter, when the snow may slow down the traffic above ground.

クイズ Hokkaido

1 ホルスタインは豊かな乳房からたっぷりのミルクを出します。
さて乳房は何個かな？
①4個 ②2個 ③1個

答え：③ 乳頭は4つありますが、乳房は大きな1つ。

Part1／Welcome to Hokkaido!

03 住宅事情 / My House

玄関の横にあるのは灯油タンクです。
The tank next to the entrance is for kerosene.

01 私の家は一戸建てです。

I live in a detached house.

02 屋根は無落雪の構造になっているため、隣の敷地に雪が落ちません。

The top of the roof is inverted so the snow will stay there and not slide off into the neighbor's yard.

03 玄関フードは、寒い風が入らないためです。

The glass-covered entrance keeps out the cold wind.

04 玄関で靴を脱いでください。

Please take off your shoes in the entrance hall.

05 家の中をご案内します。

Let me show you around the house.

06 ここは居間で、隣が食堂兼台所です。

This is the living room. Next to it is the combination dining room and kitchen.

07 この畳の部屋は仏間です。先祖の写真が飾ってあります。

We keep a family altar in this *tatami* mat room. Pictures of our ancestors are displayed here.

08 家の壁には厚い断熱材が入っているため冬でも暖かいです。

The thick insulation between the walls keeps the house warm in winter.

09 居間は床下暖房になっています。

The living room has underfloor heating.

10 家の価格は駅からの距離や広さで決まります。

The price of a house depends on its size and how far it is from the station.

11 平均的な一戸建ては2〜3千万円ぐらいです。

A standard detached house costs from 20 to 30 million yen.

12 わが家は35年ローンです。

We have a 35 year mortgage on our house.

ようこそ 住宅事情

55語ガイド

北海道の住宅は断熱材が厚くなっています。玄関フードもあり、窓は2重窓になっているので冬も暖かいです。父は雪を見ながら冷たいビールを飲み、私はTシャツ姿でアイスクリームを食べます。暖房温度を下げるべきかもしれません。

Houses in Hokkaido generally have thick insulation. The glass-covered entrance and double windows also help keep the house warm in winter. My father sometimes drinks beer looking out at the snow, while I eat ice cream in my T-shirt. Maybe we should lower the room temperature!

ナルホドA to Z

B サクランボ園でタイ人が、
「カリッとしたのはないの?」って。
柔らかなサクランボは苦手らしい。

Part1／Welcome to Hokkaido!

04 言葉 / Japanese

北海道の夕方の挨拶は「おばんです」。
"Obandesu" means "Good evening" in Hokkaido dialect.

01 日本語の簡単な挨拶を教えます。

Let me teach you some basic Japanese greetings.

02 食事の前には「いただきます」、終わったら「ごちそうさま」と言います。

Before a meal, we say *itadakimasu* and after a meal *gochisousama*.

03 「ありがとう」は感謝の言葉です。

***Arigato* means thank you.**

04 日本語を書くときは、漢字、ひらがな、カタカナの3種類の文字を使います。

Japanese is written using a combination of Chinese character or *kanji* and letters known as *hiragana* and *katakana*.

05 漢字は意味を表し、ひらがなとカタカナは音を表します。

***Kanji* letters represent meaning and *hiragana* and *katakana* the sounds of Japanese.**

06 日本で使われる漢字は約1万7千で、小学校では約千字習います。

There are a total of some 17,000 *kanji*. About 1,000 of them are taught in elementary school.

07 漢字を書いたTシャツが外国人には人気です。

T-shirts with *kanji* printed on them are popular among foreign visitors.

08 あなたが北海道弁を使うと周りの人が喜びますよ。

People will love hearing you use Hokkaido dialect.

09 役に立つ北海道の方言を一つ教えますね。

Let me teach you a popular word in Hokkaido dialect!

10 かわいい赤ちゃんを見たら「メンコイ」と言うとウケますよ。

When you see a cute baby, say *menkoi*. People will be impressed!

アイヌ民族は日本の先住民族です。北海道に昔から住んでいます。ですから、北海道の地名は80パーセント以上がアイヌ語に由来しています。アイヌ語起源でよく使われる語には、ラッコ、ハスカップ、シシャモなどがあります。19世紀半ば以降、日本各地からたくさんの人々が北海道に移住してきて、日本各地の方言が持ち込まれました。

The Ainu are the indigenous people of Japan. They have long lived in Hokkaido. More than 80% of the place names of Hokkaido derive from the Ainu language, as well as some words like *rakko*, *huskup* and *shishamo*. In the mid-19th century, people from all over Japan settled in Hokkaido, bringing words from their own dialects.

クイズ Hokkaido

2 「流氷の下の天使」と言われる「クリオネ」は北の海の人気者。ところで何の仲間？
①天使 ②貝 ③カニ

Part1／Welcome to Hokkaido!

05 血液型占い Personality and Blood Type | あなたの血液型は何型ですか？
What's your blood type?

01 日本人はすぐ血液型を聞きますよ。

Japanese may ask your blood type soon after you meet them!

02 血液型で性格判断するのが好まれているからです。

In Japan, people like to guess one's personality according to blood type.

03 血液型で人の性格が決まるなんてヘンですか？

You don't believe that blood type influences personality?

04 私の両親はAとBです。私はOで、姉はA、弟はBです。

My mother is type A and my father type B. I am O. My sister is A and my brother B.

05 A型は親切で責任感が強く、きれい好きで慎重派です。

People with blood type A are said to be kind, responsible and big on cleanliness. They like to consider things carefully.

06 B型はフレンドリーで楽観的。マイペースで人とすぐに打ち解けます。

Type B people are said to be friendly and optimistic. They like to go their own way and open their hearts to everybody.

07 O型は現実的で野心家。細かいことは気にしません。

Type O people are said to be realistic and ambitious. They don't get hung up on details.

08 AB型は繊細で複雑な性格で、理想と夢を追います。

Type AB people are said to be sensitive and have complicated personalities. They chase ideals and dreams.

日本人は占いが好きです。人気の占いには、星占い、手相、風水などがあります。神社ではおみくじを引き運勢を占います。それに迷信深いんですよ。例えば、日本の病院には4号室はありません。4が死と同じ音だからです。

Many Japanese like fortunetelling such as palm reading, astrology and feng shui. Japanese are also superstitious. For example, the number 4 is not used in hospital room numbers because its pronunciation sounds the same as the word for death.

C 「日本人はslimyな食感が好きよね〜」って言われてびっくり。
そういえばトロロ、オクラ、納豆など、外国人はどれも苦手。

Part1／Welcome to Hokkaido!

06 予定 / Plans
どこへ行きたいですか？
Where would you like to go?

01 何に興味がありますか？

What are you interested in?

02 札幌市内には定期観光バスが運行しています。

There are regular sightseeing buses in Sapporo.

03 円山動物園は子どもにも大人にも面白いですよ。

Maruyama Zoo is enjoyable for both children and adults.

04 家でゆっくりしていたいですか？

Do you want to relax at home?

05 天気が良いのでドライブに行きましょうか？

It's a beautiful day! Shall we go for a drive?

06 1時間もあれば、海、湖、山、どこへでも行けます。

In just one hour, we can get to the sea, a lake, or a mountain.

07 定山渓の温泉に行ってみますか？

How about visiting a hot spring in Jozankei?

08 市内にはたくさんサイクリングロードがありますよ。

There are many cycling roads in the city.

09 自転車も借りられます。

We can rent bikes.

10 円山でお地蔵さんを見ながらハイキングもできます。

We can hike up Mt.Maruyama, looking at the *jizo* statues along the trail.

11 山の頂上でおにぎりを食べるのは最高です。

Rice balls taste best when eaten on top of a mountain.

12 今日は雨なので、ショッピングモールに行きましょうか？

It is raining today. Should we go to a shopping mall instead?

藻岩山にロープウェイで上りましょう。まずは、市電と無料シャトルバスに乗ってロープウェイ駅まで行きます。ロープウェイに乗ると5分で中間駅。そこでケーブルカーに乗り換えて頂上に向かいます。いろいろな乗り物も楽しいですよ。頂上からは札幌市街が見渡せます。

Let's take the ropeway up to the top of Mt. Moiwa. First, we'll get on the street car, then take the free shuttle bus to the ropeway base station. From there, it's just a 5-minute ride to the mid-point station. Then we'll take a cable car to the top. Riding different cars is part of the fun! From the summit, we'll get a splendid view of Sapporo.

クイズ Hokkaido

3 北海道の湖の多くが冬は凍結するので、凍った湖でワカサギ釣りや花火大会が楽しめる。では、全面凍結しない湖はどこ？
① 阿寒湖　② 摩周湖　③ 屈斜路湖

答え：②　摩周湖、全面凍結しない。

Part1／Welcome to Hokkaido!

07 神社 / A shrine

CD-07

あれは狛犬です。
These are called stone guardian dogs.

01 近所の公園に行きましょう。

Let's go to a park in the neighborhood.

02 ブランコや滑り台、砂場があります。

There are swings, slides and a sand box.

03 犬を散歩させている人がいますね。あれは北海道犬です。

Someone is walking a dog. This breed is called a Hokkaido Dog.

04 公園の隣に神社があります。

There is a Shinto shrine next to the park.

05 神社には鳥居をくぐって入ります。

We'll enter the shrine through the *torii* gate.

06 真ん中は神様の道なので端を歩きます。

Please walk on the side. The center of the walkway is for the deities.

07 手水舎(ちょうずや)で手と口を清めましょう。

We'll have to purify our hands and mouth at the washing basin.

08 神道は日本古来の宗教です。お参りしてみますか？

Shintoism is Japan's traditional religion. Would you like to pray?

09 賽銭箱に小銭を入れます。

You can put some change in the offering box.

10 二礼二拍手一礼をします。

First bow twice, clap twice and then bow one last time.

11 この神社はパワースポットですよ。良いことがあるかもしれません。

People say this shrine has positive spiritual energy. It may bring us good luck.

12 おみくじをひいてみましょう！

You can buy a paper slip that tells your fortune.

ようこそ神社

鳥居を通って神社の境内に入ります。鳥居のそばには1対の狛犬がいます。一つは口を開けていて、これは始まりを表し、もう一つは口を閉じていて、終わりを表します。本殿に進み、礼拝する前に鈴を鳴らします。お賽銭を入れて家内安全を祈りましょう。

We'll walk into the shrine compound through the *torii* gate. Near the gate, there sit a pair of stone guardian dogs. The one with its mouth open represents the beginning, and the one with its mouth closed the end. We'll proceed to the main building and ring the bells before we pray. Throw some coins into the offering box and wish for the happiness and safety of our families!

ナルホドAtoZ

D 無落雪住宅を指さし、「5メートルも雪が降るのにこの屋根で大丈夫？」。「内側に傾斜があり、屋根で溶けて下水に」というと「WOW! This is Japan!」。

Part1／Welcome to Hokkaido!

08 コンビニ / Convenience Stores

近所のコンビニに寄りましょう。
Let's drop in at a convenience store near my house.

01 24時間開いています。

It is open 24 hours.

02 朝ごはんにおにぎりを買いましょう。

Let's buy some rice balls for breakfast.

03 おにぎりの具には鮭やシーチキン、タラコなどがあります。

At the center of a rice ball you'll find one of a number of fillings. Salmon, tuna and mayonnaise, and salted cod roe are some typical examples.

04 コメとのりの間にフィルムがはさんであるので、のりはパリッとしています。

The nori sheet wrapping stays crispy, thanks to a plastic film separating it from the rice ball.

05 おにぎりを温めてもらうのが北海道流です。

You can ask them to heat up your rice ball, Hokkaido style.

06 ガラナは北海道で人気の飲み物です。

Garana is a popular drink in Hokkaido.

07 買い物、コピー、写真のプリント、支払いをしたり、荷物を送ったりします。

People come here to shop, photocopy, print photographs, pay bills, and send parcels.

08 コンビニではトイレが使えますよ。

You can use the toilets in a convenience store.

09 ドライブマップを買っていきましょう。

I have to buy a road map.

10 ATMでお金をおろしますね。

I need to get some money at the ATM.

55語ガイド

寒いですね、コンビニで温まりましょう。このコンビニでは100円でいれたてのコーヒーが飲めるんですよ。紙コップをレジで受け取り、コーヒーマシンから自分で入れます。小腹もすきましたね。豚マンを買って、あそこのいすに座って食べましょう。体の芯から温まりますよね。

Don't you feel cold? Let's warm up in the *combini*. Here, we can buy freshly brewed coffee for just one hundred yen. When you pay, they give you a cup, then you make your own coffee at the machine. I am a bit hungry. Shall we buy a steamed pork bun and eat it on the bench over there? It will warm us up from inside.

クイズ Hokkaido

4 ソーラン節の「ソーラン」って?
①相談の方言 ②漁のかけ声 ③騒がしいこと

答え:② ニシン漁での掛け声が、踊りや歌の言葉が発祥。

Part1／Welcome to Hokkaido!

09 病気 Sickness | 風邪気味ですか？
Are you coming down with a cold?

CD-09

01 インフルエンザの予防接種は受けましたか？

Have you got a flu shot this year?

02 寒気がしますか？

Do you have a chill?

03 吐き気はありますか？

Do you feel sick?

04 薬局で薬を買いましょうか？

Do you want to buy some medicine at the pharmacy?

05 日本では熱はわきの下で測ります。

In Japan, we take our temperature under the arm.

06 熱が37.5度ありますね。

You have a temperature of 37.5 degrees.

07 近くの病院に行きましょうか？

Do you want to go to a clinic near my house?

08 処方箋をもらい薬局で薬を受け取ります。

We'll get a prescription and have it filled at a pharmacy.

09 日本人は、昔から病気の時はおかゆに梅干しを入れて食べます。

When sick, Japanese eat rice porridge with pickled plum.

10 ゆっくり休んでくださいね。

Take a rest.

11 水はたくさん飲んだ方がいいですよ。

You need to drink as much water as you can.

風邪気味ですか？　よく効く対処法を教えますね。私は足湯をしながら白湯を飲みます。汗が出て具合がよくなります。母は、のどが痛い時はハチミツ漬大根汁を飲みます。生姜湯も風邪の予防になりますよ。あなたの国では風邪気味の時はどのようにしますか？

Do you think you may have a cold? Let me share a remedy that works for me. Take a hot foot bath and sip hot water at the same time. It will make you sweat, and you'll feel better. For a sore throat, my mother makes a syrup made from honey and sliced *daikon* radish. A cup of hot ginger tea also works. What are some home remedies for colds in your country?

 セットメニューや懐石料理を
「あらかじめ組み合わせが決まっていてラクね」と言うアジア人。
「全部最初から選びたかった」と言う西洋人。違うもんだね〜。

Part1／Welcome to Hokkaido!

10 学校 Schools | 新学期は4月に始まります。
The school year starts in April.

01 見てください。グラウンドで小学生が野球をしていますよ。

Look! Primary school children are playing baseball on the school grounds.

02 小学校は6年間、中学校は3年間が義務教育です。

Children in Japan are required to attend 6 years of primary school and 3 years of junior high school.

03 ほとんどの子どもたちは近所の小・中学校に通います。

Most children go to the school nearest their home.

04 学校では遠足や運動会があります。

At school they have field trips and sports days.

05 先生にはあだ名をよくつけますよ。例えば、私の担任は「ガマガエル」でした。

We often give our teachers nicknames. My homeroom teacher's was "Toad".

06 中・高校では部活動が盛んで、生徒たちは放課後と週末に練習します。

In junior and senior high school many students participate in club activities. Most of them have practice sessions after school and on weekends.

07 入学試験のために塾に行く人が多いんですよ。

Many students study for entrance exams at special cram schools.

08 学校生活で一番楽しかったのは高校の修学旅行です。

My best memory from my school life is our high school trip.

09 私は修学旅行で広島と京都に行きました。

My class went to Hiroshima and Kyoto on our school trip.

ようこそ 学校

55語ガイド

北海道は本州より冬休みが長いんですよ。冬にはひどく吹雪く時があるので、休みが長いのはいいことだと私は思います。冬休みの間、学生はスキーを習ったり、塾に通って勉強したりします。もちろん、家族と旅行したり、家でのんびりする時間もありますよ。

Winter vacation is longer in Hokkaido than in the rest of Japan. I think it is good because there may be bad snowstorms in winter. During this long break, students study at cram schools or take ski lessons. Of course, they also have time to travel with their family or just relax at home.

クイズ Hokkaido

5 「ピリカピリカ」っていうアイヌ語の歌があるけど、ピリカってどんな意味？
① 辛い　② かわいい　③ 光っている

答え：② コメリカという名前のお店もあるよ。

Part1／Welcome to Hokkaido!

11 仕事 / Jobs
昨日は残業でした。
I worked overtime yesterday.

CD-11

01 春は転勤の季節です。

Companies transfer their employees in spring, at the end of the fiscal year.

02 転勤になると、父親が単身赴任する場合があります。

When transferred to a distant city, the father may move there alone.

03 子どもの教育や介護のためです。

The children stay behind to attend school, and the mothers to care for children and elderly relatives.

04 大学生は、3年生から就職活動を始めます。

University students start job hunting in their third year of school.

05 就職が決まるまで試験が何段階もあります。

Before being accepted by a company, a job applicant has to go through several stages of tests.

06 大学新卒者の年収は200万円ぐらいです。

The average entry level salary for college graduates is about 2 million yen a year.

07 ここ数年の失業率は4パーセント前後です。

The unemployment rate has been around 4% over the past few years.

08 ほとんどの会社は週休2日です。

Most companies have a 5-day work week.

09 日本では60から65歳でたいていの人が定年になります。

In Japan the retirement age is usually between 60 and 65.

10 定年後にボランティアや再就職をする人もいます。

Some people retire and start volunteering. Others do not retire, but find a new job instead.

11 2015年現在では、65歳から年金を受給します。

As of 2015, people 65 years and over are eligible to receive a pension.

55語ガイド

日本の大学生は3年生から就職活動を始めます。数十社にエントリーシートを出す学生もいます。希望の会社に入るのに一生懸命です。日本のバブル経済崩壊後には、氷河期と言われるほど求人が少ない時期がありました。私はそんな氷河期が二度と戻らなければいいと願っています。

In Japan, college students start job hunting in their junior year. It is not uncommon for them to send application to a dozen companies or more. They go all out to get into the company of their choice. In the past, after the bubble economy burst in Japan, there was a period called "the ice age" for new college graduates. Few jobs were available for them. I hope the ice age never comes back.

ナルホドA to Z

F 皮つきタラのグリルを見て、「皮を取って焼いたものに替えて」という西洋人。「自分で皮を取るのはイヤだから」だって。
これってわがまま？ 正当な要求？ いまだに悩む。

Part1／Welcome to Hokkaido!

12 北海道の食 / Foods in Hokkaido

新鮮な海産物が年中食べられます。
Fresh seafood is available all year round.

01 北海道は農・水産物の食材が豊富です。

Hokkaido is rich in farm and marine products.

02 日本の食料自給率は約40パーセントですが、北海道は約190パーセントです。

The food sufficiency rate in Hokkaido is about 190%, compared with only about 40% in Japan as a whole.

03 海産物では鮭、マグロ、イカ、カニなどが有名です。

Popular seafoods in Hokkaido include tuna, squid and crab.

04 寿司や刺身、海鮮丼などがおいしいですよ。

Sushi and sashimi are very delicious, as well as seafood served atop bowls of rice.

05 鮭トバやイカ珍味も人気のお土産ですよ。

Dried salmon and shredded dried squid are popular souvenirs.

06 北海道のコンブから最高のダシがとれます。

Hokkaido kelp makes the tastiest broth.

07 コンブを食べて育つウニも絶品ですよ。

Sea urchin fed on kelp tastes fantastic!

08 北海道はラーメンも名物です。

***Ramen* is one of Hokkaido's signature foods.**

09 旭川の醤油、札幌の味噌、函館の塩味など各地の代表的ラーメンがあります。

Different places have their own local *ramen* flavors: salt in Hakodate, soy sauce in Asahikawa, and *miso* in Sapporo.

| 10 | スープカレーは最近外国人に人気です。 |

Soup curry is now popular among foreign visitors.

| 11 | 農産物では、米やジャガイモ、トウモロコシ、アスパラなどが名産です。 |

Rice, potato, corn, and asparagus are some of the farm produce Hokkaido is famous for.

| 12 | ホテルの売店でも贈り物用のジャガイモやカボチャを売っています。 |

Potatoes and pumpkins are sold as gift items at hotel shops.

55語ガイド

北海道は昼夜の温度差が大きいので野菜や果物が甘くておいしいです。牛乳も乳脂肪分が高くてコクがあります。また、北海道の近海には寒流と暖流が流れ、魚の種類が多いです。おいしいものがたくさんあるので、食の王国と言われています。

The fruits and vegetables grown in Hokkaido are very sweet and delicious due to the large difference between daytime and nighttime temperatures. Hokkaido milk is also richer and tastier. And the sea currents around the island make a great variety of seafood available. For these reasons Hokkaido is often called a "food paradise."

クイズ Hokkaido

| 6 | 道産子って北海道で生まれた人のことを言うよね。でも本来は何の動物？
①シカ ②フクロウ ③ウマ |

答え：③ 北海道原産の和種馬のこと。

ようこそ 北海道の食

Part1／Welcome to Hokkaido!

13 食事 / Meals

母と私で北海道の郷土料理を作りました。
My mother and I made some Hokkaido food.

01 今日はあなたの歓迎会です。
Today we'll have a welcome party for you!

02 お祝いに赤飯を炊きました。
I cooked some steamed rice called *sekihan* for you.

03 北海道ではもち米に甘納豆を入れて作ります。
In Hokkaido we cook sweet beans in with the sticky rice.

04 ゴマ塩をかけて食べてください。
Sprinkle salt and black sesame over the rice before you eat it.

05 茶わん蒸しには栗の甘露煮が入っています。
Egg custard has sweet chestnut in it.

06 上に乗った緑の葉は三つ葉で、日本の香草です。
The green leaves are a Japanese herb called *mitsuba*.

07 タラの三平汁には白子も入っています。トロリとしていておいしいですよ。
In this cod soup, I added *shirako* or cod milt. It's creamy and delicious!

08 ホッケの開きは羅臼産です。皮も食べてくださいね。
The grilled *hokke* is from Rausu. Try the skin, too.

09 ハタハタの煮つけは小骨が多いので、気を付けてください。
When you eat cooked *hatahata* sandfish, watch out for the tiny bones.

10 昆布巻きの中には鮭を入れました。
I used salmon in the rolled kelp.

11 北海道では冬にいろいろな漬け物を食べます。

In Hokkaido, we eat a lot of pickles in winter.

12 ニシン漬けは隣の家からいただきました。

These herring and vegetable pickles were made by my neighbor.

今日は手巻きずしです。自分で作ってみてください。材料は刺身や野菜、酢飯、のりなどです。のりの上に酢飯を乗せ、その上に好きな材料を乗せてクルクル巻きます。わさび醤油につけて食べてください。私が好きなのはカイワレと納豆、シソとマグロです。うまく作れましたか？

Today, we'll make rolled sushi. You can make your own sushi. We use slices of raw fish, vegetables, vinegared rice, and *nori* sheets. First put rice on a sheet of *nori*, then put the ingredients you like on top and roll it all up. When ready, dip it in soy sauce with *wasabi* horse radish. Two of my favorites are *natto* with *kaiware* sprouts and tuna with *shiso* herb. How did yours turn out?

ナルホド A to Z

G 北海道の各地にあるクマ牧場はアジア人には大人気。
「かわいい」と餌をやる。西洋人にはブーイング。
「自然に返せ」と言う。違うもんだね〜。

Part1／Welcome to Hokkaido!

14 そば打ち / Buckwheat Noodles

ソバの花はきれいですよ。
Buckwheat flowers are beautiful!

CD-14

01 今日の昼は祖父がそばを打ちます。

My grandfather will make *soba*, or buckwheat noodles, for lunch.

02 祖父はそば打ちの教室に通っています。

He has been to a *soba* making class.

03 自分で作ると一層おいしいですよ。

***Soba* tastes better when you make it yourself.**

04 そば粉をこねて広げます。次に、薄くのばして細く切ります。

First mix buckwheat flour with water and knead the dough. Then spread the dough into a thin sheet. Finally, cut it into thin noodles.

05 そば用のコネ鉢や包丁を使います。

We use a special *soba* kneading bowl and a *soba* knife.

06 お湯でゆでて水洗いした後に、水を切って、冷たいそばつゆで食べます。

After boiling the noodles, rinse them in cold water and drain them well. Dip each bite of noodles in the cold sauce before eating them.

07 薬味はワサビとネギです。

Usual condiments are *wasabi* radish and chopped green onion.

08 そばつゆはカツオや昆布のダシから作ります。

Kelp and bonito flakes are used to make the *soba* sauce.

09 そばを食べるときはすすって食べた方がおいしいんですよ。

Slurping *soba* makes them taste more delicious!

10 北海道は全国一のそばの生産地です。

Hokkaido is Japan's number one buckwheat producing area.

そばは低カロリーなのに栄養分が豊富で健康食として人気があります。どこの家でも長寿を願って年越しにそばを食べます。引っ越してくると、近所にそばを配る家もあります。末長く仲良くしましょうという挨拶ですね。

***Soba* are a popular health food because they are nutritious and low in calories. They also symbolize a long length of time. People eat *soba* on New Year's Eve and make a wish that their lives will be long like a noodle. Some people give *soba* to their neighbors when they move into a new place, hoping they can establish a long lasting relationship with their neighbors.**

 Hokkaido

7 髪の毛が薄くなった人が引っ越したがる道北の町は？
①増毛　②名寄　③幸福

答え：①　増毛します！

Part1／Welcome to Hokkaido!

15 別れ Good Bye! | あっという間でしたね。 Time flies!

CD-15

01 さびしくなります。
I will miss you.

02 北海道は楽しかったですか？
Did you enjoy your stay in Hokkaido?

03 FacebookやLINEで連絡取り合いましょう。
Let's keep in touch on Facebook or LINE.

04 今日の夕方の飛行機ですね。
Your flight will be this evening.

05 父が車で空港まで送ります。
My father will drive you to the airport.

06 あなたのおかげであなたの国のことに興味がわきました。
Thanks to you, I am now more interested in your country.

07 英語がもっとうまくなるように頑張ります。
I will study harder to become a better English speaker.

08 今度は私があなたの国に行きます。
Next time, I will see you in your country.

09 さよなら！ また会いましょう。
Good bye! See you again!

10 無事にお帰り下さい。
Have a safe trip back home.

11 北海道にまた来てくださいね。お待ちしています。

Come back to Hokkaido again. I look forward to it.

55語ガイド

一緒に北海道を旅して楽しかったです。温泉が良かったでしょう。浴衣で登別の温泉街を歩いたのも楽しかったですよね。今度は冬に流氷や雪まつりを見に来ませんか？ 全く違う北海道が見られますよ。真っ白い雪に覆われた大地は美しいです。

I enjoyed traveling with you around Hokkaido. We had a good time at the hot spring, didn't we? Walking in *yukata* on the streets of Noboribetsu was really fun. Come back to see the drift ice and the snow festivals in winter. Hokkaido will look different. The land is beautiful covered with sparkling snow!

H　「温泉ではどう行動するの？」
　　「最初に体を洗って、5分お湯につかり、出る」
　　「次は露天風呂に10分かな」と具体的に教えると喜ばれる。

知ってるつもり アジア編❶ You Know What?

北海道を訪れるアジアからの旅行者がますます増えています。一口にアジアと言っても、国や地域によって考え方はさまざま。相手の国のことを知っていると話が弾みます。

●タイ

国土	51万4000㎢（日本の1.4倍）
人口	6593万人（2010年現在。日本の人口の約半分）
首都	バンコク
民族	タイ族75%、中国系14%のほか多数の少数民族からなる
宗教	約94%が仏教
飛行機で	札幌・東京から約6時間
日本の100円は?	約28バーツ（2014年現在）
日本が正午なら	午前10時（マイナス2時間）
こんにちは	サワッ ディー クラップ（女性は「クラップ」ではなく「カー」）
ありがとう	コップ クン クラップ （女性は「クラップ」ではなく「カー」）
Masako's view	信仰心が厚く、国王を尊敬している。日本への憧れが強く、女の子には日本風のファッションが人気。なぜか、イッセイミヤケの店に行きたがる。

●シンガポール

国土	716㎢（函館市より少し大きい）
人口	540万人（2013年現在。北海道とほぼ同じ）
首都	シンガポール
民族	中国系74%、マレー系13%、インド系9%など
宗教	仏教、イスラム教、キリスト教、ヒンズー教など
飛行機で	東京から約6時間
日本の100円は?	1.1シンガポールドル（2014年現在）
日本が正午なら	午前11時（マイナス1時間）
こんにちは	ハロー
ありがとう	サンキュー
Masako's view	北海道の大自然にあこがれ、毎年12月になると大家族で雪遊びに来る御一行様。ジーンズ姿のまま鼻水たらして子どもと戯れるお父さんに、「あんたはエラい！」。

●インドネシア

国土	190万㎢（日本の約5倍）。ジャワ、スマトラなど島多数
人口	2億4900万人（2013年現在）
首都	ジャカルタ
民族	大多数がマレー系（ジャワ人、スンダ人など）。中国系も
宗教	イスラム教87%、プロテスタント6%、カトリック4%、ヒンズー教、仏教
飛行機で	東京から約7時間
日本の100円は?	1万325ルピア（2014年現在）
日本が正午なら	午前10時（首都ジャカルタ、マイナス2時間）
こんにちは	スラマッパギ（朝） スラマッ シアン（昼） スラマッツ ソレ（夕方）
ありがとう	トゥリマ カシ
Masako's view	北海道に来るのは中国系が多いよう。出身地域によって雰囲気が全く違うのが不思議。たくさんの島がある大きい国だからかな?

Part 2

Enjoy Hokkaido Life!
[季節を感じて]

アジア人に人気の 北海道みやげベスト10 <食べ物編>
①白い恋人 ②じゃがポックル ③マルセイバターサンド ④ロイズのチョコレート ⑤さきイカ
⑥かき餅 ⑦真空パックのトウキビ ⑧メロンケーキ ⑨抹茶味のキットカット ⑩ほたて貝柱

Part2 ／ Enjoy Hokkaido Life!

16 春が来た / Spring Has Come.

4月には会社の新年度が始まります。
The new fiscal year for companies starts in April.

01 新入社員は入社式後に研修を受けます。

After the company's welcoming ceremony, newly hired employees will have to take an introductory training course.

02 研修ではビジネスマナーや丁寧な日本語を教わります。

In the training they will learn business manners and polite Japanese.

03 新しいことを始めたいと思う人が多いので、語学学習、趣味の本がたくさん売れます。

As many people want to start something new, books on foreign languages and hobbies sell well.

04 文化教室は新しい生徒であふれます。

Culture schools have dozens of new students.

05 テレビでは新しい番組が始まります。

New programs start on TV.

06 冬のコートをクリーニングに出します。ポケットに思いがけず小銭が入っていることがあり、嬉しくなることがありますよ。

I take my winter coats to a cleaner. Sometimes I am pleasantly surprised to find some spare change in the pockets!

07 冬のブーツを片付けて、夏靴を靴箱に並べます。

I put away my winter boots and put my summer shoes in the shoe closet.

08 花粉症の症状が出る人がいます。北海道ではシラカバの花粉が主な原因です。

Some people may suffer from hay fever. The major cause in Hokkaido is white birch pollen.

春 — 春が来た

峠や山にはまだ雪がありますが、近所の道路の雪は消えました。天気予報では、しばらく暖かい日が続くそうです。週末には夏タイヤに交換しようと思います。ようやく長い冬が終わりに近付いています。

Though there is still some snow left on mountain passes, the roads around my house are clear. The weather forecast says it will be warmer for the next few days. So I plan to put summer tires back on my car. The long winter has finally come to an end.

クイズ Hokkaido

8 JR北海道のICカード「kitaca」のキャラクターは何の動物？
① エゾリス　② エゾナキウサギ　③ エゾモモンガ

答え：⑧　名前のICカードキャラクターはエゾモモンガ！

Part2／Enjoy Hokkaido Life!

17 桜 Cherry Blossoms
CD-17

桜が満開！
Cherry blossoms are in full bloom!

01 桜は日本を代表する花です。100円硬貨には桜の絵が描かれています。

Cherry blossoms are the national flower of Japan. They are depicted on 100-yen coins.

02 桜が満開になると、桜の木全体がピンク色に見えます。

When the cherry blossoms come into full bloom, the entire tree looks pink.

03 雨や風で一斉に桜の花びらが散ると、地面はピンク色のカーペットのように見えます。

When the petals fall to the ground after rain or strong wind, the ground looks like a pink carpet.

04 日本で見られる桜は200種類ほどです。一番多いのはソメイヨシノで、全体の80パーセントを占めます。

There are 200 different kinds of cherry blossoms seen in Japan. Among them *Somei Yoshino* is the most common, accounting for 80 % of the total.

05 ソメイヨシノは、北海道の寒い地域では育ちません。

***Somei Yoshino* trees don't grow in the colder regions of Hokkaido, however.**

06 北海道では千島桜、エゾ山桜などの桜が咲きます。

The cherries of Hokkaido include the *Chishima* and the *Ezoyama* varieties.

07 テレビでは各地の桜の開花状況が流れます。

The progress of the cherries, as they blossom in various places, is reported on TV.

08 桜の開花は、沖縄が2月、東京で3月、北海道では5月初めごろです。

The cherry blossoms start in Okinawa in February, reach Tokyo in March, and finally Hokkaido in early May.

春
桜

09 北海道には函館、静内、松前など桜の名所がたくさんあります。

Hakodate, Shizunai, and Matsumae are some of the famous cherry blossom viewing spots in Hokkaido.

10 桜の季節には桜のケーキや桜アイスクリームなどが出回ります。

This season features cakes and ice creams, flavored with cherry blossoms.

北海道では5月になると山の木々が新緑に色づき始めます。モクレン、スイセン、レンギョウ、ツツジに続き、梅や芝桜も咲きます。またたく間に、モノクロの風景から色鮮やかな景色へと劇的に変化します。

In May, fresh leaves color the mountains green in Hokkaido. Japanese magnolia, daffodils, forsythias, azaleas, plums and pink moss come into bloom in procession. Almost overnight, the bleak winter scenery is replaced by the brightly colored scenery of spring.

ナルホド A to Z

I　目薬、ハンドクリーム、フェイスパック——
これ、なんだと思う？
答えは近ごろ人気の日本みやげ。

Part2 ／ Enjoy Hokkaido Life!

18 夏の楽しみ / Summer Days
ビアガーデンがにぎわっています！ / Beer gardens are bustling with people.

01 暑い日はガラス窓を開けて網戸にします。

On hot days, I open the glass door and let the air in through the screen door.

02 地下鉄車内の風鈴の音が涼しげです。

The wind chimes in subway cars make the air feel cooler.

03 デパートや地下街では、節電のために冷房温度を高めに設定します。

Department stores and underground shopping malls turn their thermostats up to save electricity on air conditioning.

04 会社員はネクタイとジャケットなしで仕事をします。

Office workers go without ties and jackets.

05 夏には、ラーメン屋さんのメニューに冷やし中華が登場します。

In summer, cold Chinese noodles appear on the menus of *ramen* restaurants.

06 暑い日にはかき氷やアイスキャンディーがよく売れます。

On hot days, shaved ice and popsicles sell well.

07 夕方になると野外のビアガーデンがにぎわいます。

In the evening, open air beer gardens fill up with people.

08 私は暑い日には熱いラーメンかカレーを食べて、暑気払いをします。

On hot days, I eat hot *ramen* or curry to forget the summer heat.

09 夏の夜に、廃屋や病院などの心霊スポットめぐりをする人もいます。

Some people like to visit old haunted houses or abandoned hospitals to feel a chill on summer evenings.

10 お盆には、テレビでホラー映画や怪談を放送します。

During the Bon festival, horror movies and scary stories are often broadcast on TV.

11 ホラー映画を見ると恐くて夜にトイレに行けないことがあります。

After watching a horror movie, I sometimes get too scared to go to the bathroom.

夏と言えばビール！ 北海道の地ビールがおいしいです。暑い日は、仕事帰りに会社の同僚とビアガーデンでビールをグイッ。ギンギンに冷えたビールと枝豆が最高ですね。

No summer is complete without beer! We can enjoy good local beers. On hot summer nights, after work, I often go to an open air beer garden with my colleagues and down a few cold ones. Nothing beats a pitcher of ice-cold beer with some green *edamame* soybeans on the side!

クイズ Hokkaido

9 帯広など十勝地方で有名な温泉の泉質は？
① メール泉　② モール泉　③ ゴール泉

答え：②　植物からの有機質がたっぷり！

19 お盆 / Bon Festival

盆踊りはだれでも参加できます。
Anyone can join in the Bon Dance!

01 お盆には先祖の霊が帰ってくると言われています。

It is believed that during the Bon Festival, the spirits of our ancestors return to earth.

02 家族が集まり、墓参りをします。

Family members get together and pay a visit to the graves of their ancestors.

03 線香やロウソク、花、お菓子、果物を先祖の墓に供えます。

There they make offerings of incense, candles, flowers, sweets and fruits.

04 帰省客で列車や飛行機が満席になります。

Trains and airplanes are packed with people returning to their hometowns.

05 道路は車で渋滞します。

The roads are also jammed with cars.

06 お盆には学校の同窓会が開催されます。

During the Bon Festival, school reunions are often held.

07 夜には公園で盆踊りが行われます。

Bon Dances are held in parks at night.

08 浴衣を着て踊っている人がいます。涼しげですね。

Some people dance in their *yukata*. It looks cool.

09 盆踊りは簡単な踊りです。私たちも踊りましょう！

Bon Dances are easy to learn. Let's join in.

10 札幌では大通公園で盆踊りが行われ、だれでも参加できます。

Everyone is free to join in the Bon Dances held in Sapporo's Odori Park.

11 綿あめ、金魚すくいの露店が出ます。

At some stalls you can buy cotton candy. At others you can try your luck at scooping up goldfish.

お盆には休暇を取って故郷に帰り、実家の墓参りをします。親戚や幼なじみと久しぶりに再会します。この時期には、小中学校の同窓会も開かれます。私は初恋の人に会って、昔を思い出して胸がときめきました。

During the Bon Festival, I take a few days off and return to my hometown to pay a visit to my ancestors' grave. It's good to see relatives and old friends I haven't seen in a while. Elementary and junior high schools sometimes hold reunions. Once I ran into my first love at one of those, and my heart fluttered.

ナルホド A to Z

J 「生まれた曜日は?」と聞かれ「??」。
タイ人ならみんな知っているそうだけど、
日本人はたいてい知らないよね〜。

Part2 / Enjoy Hokkaido Life!

20 食欲の秋 / Autumn Foods
北海道のトウキビとジャガイモは最高！
Corn and potatoes in Hokkaido are the best!

CD-20

01 北海道のトウキビが甘いのは昼夜の気温差が大きいためです。

The big difference between day time and night time temperatures makes corn grown in Hokkaido especially sweet.

02 生でも食べられます。

Some corn can even be eaten raw.

03 トウキビチョコレートとトウキビアイスが人気です。

Corn chocolate and corn ice cream are also popular.

04 北海道はトウキビとジャガイモの生産量が日本一です。毎年、新しい品種が開発されています。

Hokkaido is the number one producer of both corn and potatoes. And new varieties are developed every year.

05 白、黄色、紫色のジャガイモがあり、味や食感、色が違います。

Potatoes come in different flavors, textures, and colors. There are white, yellow and purple potatoes.

06 北海道では、ゆでたジャガイモにバターか塩辛をのせて食べます。

In Hokkaido we eat boiled potatoes with butter or pickled squid.

07 イモモチやポテトコロッケがコンビニで売られています。

You can buy potato dumplings and potato croquettes at convenience stores.

北海道にはいろいろな種類のトウキビがあります。モチモチした食感のものや甘みの強いもの、白いもの、生で食べられるものなどです。どれも食べてみてください。札幌大通公園では、トウキビワゴンが人気で、ゆでたのと焼いたのを売っています。私たちもいただきましょうか？

秋

食欲の秋

There are various kinds of corn produced in Hokkaido. Some have a chewy texture, some are sweeter, some are white, and some can be eaten raw. You have to try them all. At Sapporo Odori Park, they sell grilled or boiled corn on the cob. Would you like to try some?

クイズ Hokkaido

10 いつも自慢げな道央の湖は？
① 洞爺湖　② 支笏湖　③ ウトナイ湖

答え：① 「トーヤ！」と自分を讃えている（「どうだ」を「どや」という関西弁もある）

21 晩秋 / Late Autumn

昨日、公園にクマが出ました。
Yesterday, a bear was spotted in the park.

01 北海道には2千から3千頭の野生のヒグマがいると言われています。

About 2,000 to 3,000 wild brown bears are estimated to live in Hokkaido.

02 ヒグマは日本にすむ熊の中では一番大きく、大人のオスは体重が500kgにもなります。

The brown bear is the largest bear in Japan. An adult male can weigh as much as 500 kg.

03 冬眠前にヒグマは餌をたくさん食べます。

The brown bear eats a lot before going into hibernation.

04 秋には市街地でヒグマが目撃されることがあります。

In autumn, bears can occasionally be sighted within the city limits.

05 クマが目撃された公園や登山道は、安全確認ができるまで閉鎖されます。

When this happens, the park or mountain path where the bear was seen is closed until it has been confirmed that the bear has left the area.

06 山にハイキングに行く時はリュックに鈴を付け、クマが近付いてこないようにします。

When we go hiking in the mountains, we attach a bell to our backpack to alert the bears to our presence.

07 クマに出会っても、死んだふりをすれば助かるといいますが、本当でしょうか？

If you do happen to run into a bear, they say you can save yourself by playing dead. I wonder if it works, though?

08 北海道では9月から紅葉が見られます。見に行きませんか？

In Hokkaido, the autumn colors begin in September. Why don't we go and see them?

09 秋になると、料理に紅葉を添えて季節感を出します。

Autumn leaves are sometimes placed on Japanese dishes to give the feeling of the season.

秋 / 晩秋

昨日、札幌市内の公園でクマが目撃されました。その公園には、「クマ目撃！」の警告版が立てられました。市の中心部に近かったので、市民はショックを受けました。これから1週間は、小学生の登校時には親が付き添います。

Yesterday, a bear was sighted in a park in Sapporo. So they put up a warning sign saying "Bear sighted here!" As the park is close to the city center, the citizens were shocked. For the next week, local parents will have to accompany their children to school.

ナルホド A to Z

K 辛い物が好きなアジア人が多い。ワサビを追加でもらっても、「小豆大じゃなくて、プラム大でくださーい！」とさらに追加を頼むハメになる。

Part2 ／ Enjoy Hokkaido Life!

22 冬の始まり / The Beginning of Winter

吐く息が白いですね。
I can see my breath!

01 あの白い雪のような虫は雪虫と呼ばれています。

That white bug that looks like a tiny snowflake is called a snow bug.

02 雪虫が姿を現して2週間後には、初雪が降ると言われています。

They say the first snowfall will come two weeks after the snow bugs make their appearance.

03 車には冬用タイヤを着用しなければなりません。

In winter, we have to put snow tires on our cars.

04 私はガソリンスタンドでタイヤ交換をしてもらいます。

I will have my tires changed at a gas station.

05 北国仕様の車はバッテリーが大容量で、フロントガラスに雪や氷を解かすための熱線が入っています。

Cars in cold areas like Hokkaido need a larger battery. Heating wires are installed inside the windshield to melt snow and ice.

06 雪道ではスリップ事故がたくさん起きるので、夏よりスピードを落として走ります。

Icy roads cause many accidents. We have to drive a lot slower than in summer.

07 ナワとムシロで庭木の冬囲いをします。木が雪の重さで折れたり、寒さで凍ったりするのを防ぐためです。

Tree branches can break under the weight of heavy snow. We bind the trees and shrubs in our gardens with straw ropes and cover them in matting.

08 初雪は10月頃で、早ければ11月末には根雪になります。

The first snow will come in October, but it doesn't start to settle until late November at the earliest.

雪虫が姿を現しました。そろそろ、自家用車を冬タイヤに交換します。庭木の冬囲いもしなければなりません。越冬野菜も買いますよ。ベランダに干しているのは、漬け物用の大根とカブです。この時期は冬支度に大忙しです。

I saw some snow bugs. I have to change the tires on my car to winter tires. I also have to tie up the tree branches in my yard. I will go and buy some vegetables for winter. The turnips and *daikon* radish on the railing of the veranda are for pickling. There are so many things that need to be done to prepare for winter around this time of year.

冬 / 冬の始まり

 Hokkaido

11 北海道の道路標識に出てこない動物は？
① 鹿　② キツネ　③ ヤンバルクイナ

答え：③ 沖縄のクイナ！

Part2 / Enjoy Hokkaido Life!

23 雪 / Snow

雪は空からのラブレター。
Snow is a love letter from the sky.

01 「雪は空からのラブレター」と有名な研究者が言いました。

A famous scientist once mused, "Snow is a love letter from the sky."

02 降ってきた雪の結晶の状態で、上空の気温や湿度がわかるからです。

The shapes of snow crystals reveal the temperature and humidity of the sky, he said.

03 道産子は雪が降っても傘は差しません。雪がサラサラで服がぬれないからです。

People in Hokkaido don't use umbrellas when it snows. The snow is dry and doesn't stick, so your clothes don't get wet.

04 年間積雪量は札幌で約5メートル、ニセコでは約11メートルもあります。

The annual snowfall is 5 meters in Sapporo and as much as 11 meters in Niseko.

05 赤と白の矢印のついた棒が道路端に立っているのが見えますか? あの矢印のおかげで、ひどい吹雪の日でも道路の端がわかるのです。

Can you see the red and white arrows above the road? Thanks to them, even in a bad snow storm, we can tell where the edge of the road is.

06 冬期間は通行止めになる道路があります。

Some roads are closed to traffic during the winter.

07 北海道では体育の授業でスキーかスケートを習います。雪の降る地域はスキー、あまり雪が降らない地域ではスケートの授業です。

In Hokkaido we all learn either skiing or skating in PE class as children. Skiing is for areas with a lot of snow and skating for the rest.

08 この公園ではスノーシューで雪の森を歩き、野外彫刻を見ることができます。雪の上にはいろいろな動物の足跡がありますよ。

In this park, we can walk on the deep snow in snowshoes and enjoy the sculpture garden. You can often see footprints of animals on the snow.

冬
雪

55語ガイド

冬になると、北海道の大地はすっかり純白の雪で覆われ、日中の気温が3度以下になります。しっかり防寒対策をして出かけましょう。使い捨てカイロを背中に貼り、手袋をして帽子をかぶり、ダウンジャケットを着れば万全です！

In winter, the vast landscape of Hokkaido becomes completely covered with snow. Daytime temperatures fall to 3℃ or under 0℃. You have to protect yourselves from the cold. Put a heat pack on your back. And make sure to wear gloves, a cap, and a down jacket. Now you are ready to go out!

ナルホドA to Z

L
「お湯ください」「お茶ですか？」「お湯ください」
「えっ？ 水じゃなくて？」。レストランで繰り返される問答。
お湯が飲みたいアジア人は多い。

Part2 ／ Enjoy Hokkaido Life!

24 大晦日 New Year's Eve

おせち料理を食べます。
We eat New Year's dishes.

CD-24

01 新年を迎えるためにいろいろな準備があります。

There are many things to be done to get ready for the New Year.

02 お歳暮を贈る人が多いので、デパートには特設コーナーができます。

Many people give year-end gifts. Department stores have a whole floor set aside for this.

03 年賀状を書き、投函します。

We also have to write and post New Year's cards.

04 新聞やテレビでは、この年の十大ニュースが発表されます。

On newspapers and TV, they announce the top ten news items of the year about to end.

05 家の大掃除をして新年を迎えます。

We try to clean our house spotless to welcome the New Year.

06 お正月用の生け花としめ縄を飾ります。

People display fresh flower arrangements and a traditional straw rope decoration called a *shimenawa*.

07 おせちは正月用の特別の料理で、それぞれの料理には家族の健康、長寿、幸運などの願いが込められています。

***Osechi* refers to special foods eaten during the New Year's holidays. Each food in *osechi* represents a different aspect of the health, longevity and happiness to be wished for in the coming year.**

08 自分で作る人もいますが、私はデパートでおせち料理を買います。

Some people still make *osechi* themselves, but I always buy mine at a department store.

09 スキー場で新年を迎える人がいます。

Some people stay at a ski resort and celebrate New Year's Day there.

10 夜食には家族そろって年越しそばを食べます。

Around midnight on New Year's Eve, we have buckwheat noodles.

55語ガイド

大晦日には子どもたちが帰省して、みんなで年取りをします。食卓にはおすしやおせち料理が並びます。和歌山県出身の義理の娘は、大晦日におせち料理を食べる北海道の習慣に驚きました。実家ではおせちは元旦から食べるのだそうです。

On New Year's Eve, we celebrate the coming of a new year together with our children. A feast of sushi and *osechi* are laid out on the table. My daughter-in-law, who is from Wakayama Prefecture, was surprised to see *osechi* on New Year's Eve. Back home, her family eats *osechi* only during the first three days of the new year. But up here in Hokkaido we start a day early.

クイズ Hokkaido

12 北海道の道路の端に立っている紅白棒は何のため？
①除雪範囲　②急こう配　③路肩弱し

答え：① 除雪の目印となる標識。

Part2 / Enjoy Hokkaido Life!

25 お正月 / New Year's Holidays

神社へ初詣に行きます。
We pay the first visit of the year to a shrine.

01 元旦には家族全員で初詣に行きます。

On New Year's Day, my family all go together to pay their first visit to a shrine.

02 お屠蘇(とそ)という薬草入りの酒を飲み健康を願います。

We drink our health with a traditional herbal sake called *o-toso*.

03 子どもたちには特別の封筒に入れてお年玉をあげます。

We give gifts of money to children in a special envelope.

04 元旦には年賀状が配達されます。

New Year's cards are delivered on New Year's Day.

05 親戚が集まり百人一首をします。

My family and relatives play the traditional card game called One Hundred Famous Poems.

06 元旦はほとんどの店が閉まっています。

Most shops are closed on New Year's Day.

07 初売りの日には、福袋目当てにデパートに行列ができます。

On the first business day of the year, department stores sell New Year's lucky bags. Many people stand in line to get one.

08 多くの会社は年末から1月3日までは休みです。

Most offices are closed during the first three days of the new year.

09 1月4日には札幌中央卸売市場で初セリがあります。

On January 4th, the first auctions of the year are held at Sapporo Central Wholesale Market.

10　初セリでは新年のご祝儀として、品物に高い値が付きます。

To celebrate the start of the new year, some items are auctioned off at higher prices.

元旦にはお雑煮を食べます。これはお餅、野菜、肉の入ったスープです。日本では地方ごとに材料と味付けが違います。全国からの移住者が多い北海道のお雑煮は、各家庭でさまざまです。私の家は餅と鶏肉とシイタケが入った醤油味です。

On the first day of the year, we eat *ozoni* soup. Each region in Japan has its own flavors and special ingredients, but all contain rice cakes, vegetables and some meat. There are many varieties of *ozoni* cooked in Hokkaido because people settled here from all over the country. My family's *ozoni* features chicken and *shiitake* mushrooms, and is flavored with soy sauce.

ナルホド A to Z

| **M** | ホッケ焼き定食を前にした米国人。
おはしは無理。
結局フォークとナイフでホッケの開きに四苦八苦。 |

Part2 / Enjoy Hokkaido Life!

26 雪仕事 / Snow Shoveling

雪かきはいい運動です！
Snow shoveling is good exercise!

01 毎晩、寝る前にテレビで降雪予報を見ます。

Every night, I watch the snow forecast on TV before going to bed.

02 雪が降るという予報が出たら、早起きして除雪をします。

When snow is forecasted, I always get up early to shovel snow.

03 札幌市は除雪に年間約130億円を使います。

The city of Sapporo spends 13 billion yen each winter on snow removal.

04 公共施設や道路の除雪は公共機関が行います。

The city removes snow from roads and around public facilities.

05 家と車庫の前の雪かきは自分でします。時間がかかりますよ。

I remove snow in front of my house and garage. It takes a lot of time.

06 積もった雪は、家の裏庭に"ママさんダンプ"で運びます。

I haul the snow to the backyard using a large snow shovel called a "mama's snow dump".

07 隣の家では機械で雪を溶かします。燃油代が高いそうです。

My neighbor uses a snow melting device. It's convenient, but the fuel is expensive.

08 屋根に雪が積もると重さで家が傷むので、時々雪下ろしをします。

I sometimes remove snow from the roof of my house so that the weight of the snow doesn't cause damage to my house.

09 除雪の時は重ね着をします。熱くなったら脱いで調節します。

I wear layered clothing for snow shoveling. When I start to feel hot, I just remove a layer.

55語ガイド

大雪や吹雪の時はどの車もノロノロ運転で、道路が渋滞します。学校が休みになることもあります。高速道路が閉鎖されたり、50キロ制限になったりします。飛行機が欠航することもあります。あなたの帰る日は吹雪かないといいですね。

A heavy snowfall or blizzard may slow down the traffic and cause traffic jams. Sometimes school classes are even canceled. The expressways can be closed or lower their speed limit to 50 kilometers per hour, and flights can be canceled too. I hope there will not be a snowstorm on the day of your departure from here.

冬 / 雪仕事

 Hokkaido

13 北海道の人気みやげ「白い恋人」の缶に描かれている山は？
① 手稲山 　② 羊蹄山 　③ 利尻富士

答え：③ 利尻島のなかばそびえ立つ利尻フジ。

Part2 / Enjoy Hokkaido Life!

27 冬祭り / Winter Festivals

各地でさまざまな冬の祭りがあります。
There are various winter festivals all over Hokkaido.

01 札幌や旭川の雪まつりでは大雪像がつくられます。

Huge snow statues are made at winter festivals in Sapporo and Asahikawa.

02 自衛隊と市民が参加して雪像を制作します。

Self-Defense Force members and citizens participate in making the snow statues.

03 郊外から純白の雪が運ばれて雪像になります。

Fresh snow is brought in from the outlying areas and used to make the statues.

04 支笏湖や層雲峡の氷祭りでは、氷像がさまざまな色でライトアップされます。

At the ice festivals at Lake Shikotsu and Sounkyo, ice statues are lit up in various colors.

05 オホーツク海沿岸の街では厳寒期に流氷祭りが行われます。

In coastal towns along the Okhotsk Sea, drift ice festivals are held in the coldest months.

06 阿寒湖では凍った湖の上で花火大会が行われます。

Fireworks displays are held on frozen Lake Akan.

07 レーザー光線やイルミネーションを楽しむ冬の祭りがあります。

Some winter festivals feature laser beam shows or light illuminations.

08 雪で作ったステージでは歌やダンスのショーがあります。

Shows with dancing and singing are held on snow stages.

09　どの冬祭りでも温かい食べ物を売っています。うどんや肉マン、ココアなどが人気です。

At any winter festival, you will find something hot to eat or drink. ***Udon*** **noodles, steamed meat buns and hot chocolate are some of the most popular items.**

10　甘酒は酒粕に砂糖を加えた温かい飲み物です。体が温まりますよ！

Amazake**, a drink of sweetened sake lees, is good for warming you up.**

層雲峡氷瀑まつりは石狩川河川敷で行われ、大氷像や滑り台があります。ライトアップされる夕方に見に行きましょう！　靴には滑り止めゴムを付けてくださいね。交差点には袋に入った砂がおいてあります。滑りそうな場所にまいて、その上を歩いてください。

Sounkyo Hyobaku Festival is held on the banks of the Ishikari River. There are huge ice statues and ice slides. Let's go see them in the evening when they are lit up. Make sure you put anti-slip rubber bands on your shoes. At pedestrian crossings, you will also find bags of sand to spread over icy spots before you walk on them.

冬　冬祭り

N	「バニラじゃなくてミルク味」。ソフトクリーム好きのリピーターさんいわく「北海道のミルクアイスは世界一」。

Part2／Enjoy Hokkaido Life!

28 春を待つ Waiting for Spring

CD-28

送別会のシーズンです。
The season for farewell parties.

01 3月には学校の卒業式が行われます。

In March, schools hold their graduation ceremonies.

02 高校や大学の入試合格者の発表があります。

High schools and colleges announce the results of their entrance examinations.

03 高校に合格した学生は、学校指定の制服を注文します。

Students who have passed their entrance exams will buy uniforms for their new schools.

04 制服が有名デザイナーによるおしゃれなものだと学校の人気が上がります。

The popularity of a school soars when its uniform is a cute one designed by a famous designer.

05 卒業後、たくさんの高校生が進学や就職で北海道を離れます。

Many high school graduates leave Hokkaido to study or work.

06 学生は友達と送別会をしたり卒業記念旅行に行ったりします。レストランやホテルはとても混み合います。

To celebrate their graduation, students have parties or take trips together. Restaurants and hotels are very crowded.

07 3月は官庁や多くの企業で人事異動が行われます。

Many companies and government offices transfer their employees in March.

08 引っ越し業者や不動産屋さんは大忙しです。引っ越しをするときは早めに見積もりを取り、業者を予約しましょう。

Moving companies and real estate agents are very busy. If you know you'll be moving in March, you have to get an estimate and book a moving van in advance.

09 花屋さんでは花束がたくさん売れます。転勤者や退職者への別れの贈り物に使われます。

Bouquets of flowers are in great demand at flower shops. They are typical gifts given to those transferred or retiring.

冬

春を待つ

55語ガイド

学生は、卒業すると同級生になかなか会えなくなります。だから、3月に友達と卒業記念旅行へ行きます。みんなで近くの温泉に泊まり、夜中までカラオケやおしゃべりを楽しみます。北海道はまだ寒いので、暖かいグアム島や沖縄へ行く人もいます。

After graduation, students will have fewer chances to be with their friends. So in March they travel together. Some go to a nearby hot spring resort. They chat and sing karaoke late into the night. As it is still cold at this time in Hokkaido, some even travel to warm places like Guam or Okinawa.

クイズ Hokkaido

14 黒いダイヤは石炭、黄色いダイヤは数の子。
では北海道名産の「赤いダイヤ」とは？
①サクランボ　②アズキ　③トマト

答え：②　全国の4分の3が北海道産です。

Part2 ／ Enjoy Hokkaido Life!

29 セグウェイ / Segway
環境に優しい乗り物です。
An environmentally friendly vehicle

01 恵庭や富良野の美しい自然の中で、セグウェイに乗ることができます。

You can ride a Segway amidst the beautiful nature of Eniwa and Furano.

02 セグウェイは電動式の乗り物で、最高20キロの速度が出ます。

A Segway is an electric vehicle. It can reach a speed of 20 km per hour.

03 まずは実際に操作してみましょう。

Let's try riding one.

04 スイッチを入れて起動させ、セグウェイの台に直立姿勢で乗ります。

Switch it on and stand upright on the Segway platform.

05 前進したいときは台の前の方に重心をかけ、後退したい時は後ろに体重をかけます。

You command the Segway to go forward by shifting your weight forward on the platform, and backward by shifting your weight backward.

06 右か左に曲がりたい時は、曲がりたい方にハンドルを向けます。

If you want to make a turn, just move the handle in the direction you want to go.

07 重心を中心に置くと、スピードが鈍ります。

If you keep your weight in the center, the Segway will slow down.

08 進行方向と逆に重心を移動させると止まります。

When you shift your weight in the opposite direction to the moving direction, it will stop.

55語ガイド

セグウェイに乗ると、わずか2、3分でこの広い公園の端まで行けます。芝生、舗装道路、砂利道も走れます。坂道も上ります。エンジン音もしないし、排気ガスも出しません。環境に優しい乗り物です。

The Segway will take you across this huge park in only two or three minutes. The Segway can move on lawns, paved roads, gravel and hills. The engine produces no noise or exhaust gas. It is an environmentally friendly vehicle.

ナルホド A to Z

O 日本のハイテクトイレ、入ったきりなかなか出てこない。「大丈夫ですか？」と声をかけたら、「どうやって流すの？」。うーん、あるある。

Part2／Enjoy Hokkaido Life!

30 野球観戦 / Watching a Baseball Game

札幌ドームで野球を見ましょう！
Let's watch a baseball game at Sapporo Dome.

01 北海道にはサッカーと野球のプロチームがあり、どちらのチームにも熱狂的なファンがいます。

We have both a professional soccer team and a professional baseball team here in Sapporo. Both have enthusiastic fans.

02 あなたの国で人気のプロスポーツは何ですか？

What professional sports are popular in your country?

03 2002年に札幌ドームでサッカー・ワールドカップの試合が行われました。

In 2002, some World Cup soccer games were held in Sapporo Dome.

04 札幌ドームの試合では、野球は人工芝、サッカーは天然芝を使います。必要に応じて入れ替わるのです。

In Sapporo Dome, baseball games are played on an artificial turf, while football games are held on a grass pitch that slides into and out of the stadium, as needed.

05 日本ハムファイターズのナイターに行きましょう。コンビニでチケットを買ってあります。札幌ドームは地下鉄駅から歩いてすぐです。

Let's go see a night game of the Nippon Ham Fighters. I've already got tickets at a convenience store. Sapporo Dome is just a short walk from the nearest subway station.

06 席に着く前にお弁当とお茶を買いましょう。私は応援グッズを買います。

On our way to our seats, let's get a boxed *bento* and a bottle of tea. I'll also buy some fan goods.

07 タンクを背負った売り子さんがビールを売りにきましたよ。飲みたいですか？

Here comes a beer vendor with a beer tank on her back. Would you like to have some?

08 応援席では、ユニフォームを着込んだ人たちが、旗を振りながら応援歌を歌っています。

In the stands, fans in their team's uniform are singing fan songs and waving cheering flags to root on the team.

09 今年は絶対にファイターズに優勝してほしいです！

I am dying to see the Fighters win the national championship this year!

70語ガイド

日本にはプロ野球の球団が12あり、全国高校野球大会で活躍した選手がたくさん入団します。プロ野球と同じぐらい高校野球は人気で、テレビの視聴率が高いんです。北海道の学校が上位に勝ち進むと、街頭のスクリーンにチームの試合が放映されます。

There are 12 professional baseball teams in Japan. The best high school baseball players join a team after graduation, especially those who did well in the All Japan High School Baseball Tournaments. These tournaments are really popular, and many people watch the games on TV. When local Hokkaido teams keep winning and move on to the top group, their games are shown on big TV screens downtown.

クイズ Hokkaido

15 道東の野付湾で行われる名物のシマエビ漁で使われるのはどんな舟？
①打瀬舟　②高瀬舟　③屋形舟

答え：① 帆かけ舟を使って、自然を傷つけずに漁をします。

Part2 / Enjoy Hokkaido Life!

31 アイスクリーム作り / Ice Cream Making

CD-31

新鮮なミルクでアイスクリームを作りましょう。

Let's make ice cream from fresh milk!

01 今日はアイスクリームをつくります。

Today, we'll make some ice cream.

02 まずはエプロンをして、手を消毒してください。

First, you should put on an apron and sanitize your hands.

03 ワッフル生地の材料でアイスクリームを入れるコーンをつくっておきます。

We will first make ice cream cones using waffle batter.

04 アイスの材料になる牛乳、生クリーム、砂糖を小さな金属ボウルに入れます。

Put all the ingredients-milk, fresh cream and sugar-in a small stainless bowl.

05 大きいボウルに氷と塩と水を入れます。金属ボウルに入った材料を冷やすためです。

In a large bowl, put some ice, salt and water. This will be used to cool the ingredients in the stainless bowl.

06 大きいボウルの中央に小さいボウルを置きます。

Put the small bowl in the center of the large bowl.

07 泡立て器で小さいボウルの材料をかき混ぜます。最初は勢いよく、細かい泡が出来てきたらゆっくりです。

Mix the ingredients in the small bowl. First, beat it vigorously until fine foam is formed. Then beat it slowly.

08 材料がボウルの中で固まったら出来上がり。

When the ingredients in the small bowl have become solid, it is done.

09 ヘラでアイスクリームをすくい、コーンにのせます。さあ、召し上がれ！

Using a spatula, place the ice cream on the cone and enjoy it!

55語ガイド

見てください！ 北海道らしい風景ですよ。たくさんのホルスタインが野原で草を食んでます。隣にはログハウスの売店があります。牛のイラストの看板がかわいいですね。「搾りたて牛乳ソフトクリーム」の旗が店の前に立っています。

Look! This is typical Hokkaido scenery. Many Holstein cows are grazing on a pasture. The log cabin on the side is a gift shop. The picture of a cow on the shop sign looks cute. The flag in front of the shop says "Ice cream made from the freshest milk".

ナルホドA to Z

P 「日本の音楽が聴きたい」と言うので
「民謡？ 琴？」と聞くと、
「いま流行ってる普通の音楽がいい」って。

Part2 ／ Enjoy Hokkaido Life!

32 果物狩り / Fruit Picking

サクランボ狩りは楽しいですよ！
It's fun to pick cherries!

01 北海道にはたくさんの果樹園があります。

There are many orchards in Hokkaido.

02 サクランボやイチゴ、リンゴ、ブドウなどの果物狩りができます。

We can pick cherries, strawberries, apples and grapes.

03 今日はサクランボ狩りに行きましょう。

Let's enjoy picking cherries today.

04 入り口で800円の入場料を払います。食べ放題ですよ。

We'll pay the fee of 800 yen at the entrance. We can eat as much as we want to.

05 日当たりのいいところのサクランボが甘いです。

Cherries growing in the sun are sweeter.

06 高いところは梯子に上ってもぎとります。

You need to use a ladder to pick the cherries on the branches up high.

07 枝には来年の芽がついていますから、傷つけないようにね。

Be careful not to hurt the buds on the branch. They will grow into cherries next year.

08 8月にはブルーベリー狩りができます。

In August, blueberry farms are open for picking.

09 ブルーベリーの実は成熟すると、緑色から明るい水色、そして紫色に変化します。濃い紫色の実が甘いですよ。

Blueberries look green when young, but turn to light blue and then purple as they mature. Dark purple blueberries are sweeter.

10 摘んだブルーベリーはジャムにしましょう。

We'll pick some blueberries to make jam.

11 売店では梨とプルーン、ラズベリーを売っています。

At the gift shop, they sell fresh fruits such as prunes, pears, and raspberries.

仁木町のフルーツ街道には野菜や果物の直売所が並んでいます。春から秋まで、新鮮な野菜や果物が安く買えます。近くには果物狩りのできる果樹園があります。私が毎年行くのは家族経営のブルーベリー園です。そこのブルーベリーパイがおいしいですよ。

Roadside stands line the Fruit Road in the town of Niki. From spring to autumn, fresh vegetables and fruits are available at reasonable prices. In this area some orchards offer fruit picking. Every year, I visit a family-run blueberry farm. The blueberry pie they make is really delicious!

Hokkaido

16 北海道の七夕は8月7日。子どもたちが「出さないとかっちゃく（ひっかく）ぞー」って、いったい何を？
① かぎ　② ろうそく　③ くさり

答え：② そもそも、ネブタとこの行事が重なるらしい。

Part2 ／ Enjoy Hokkaido Life!

33 スキー場 / Ski Areas
パウダースノーです。
It's powder snow!

01 雪道のドライブには慣れていないので、スキー場へはバスで行きましょう。

I am not used to driving on snow. Let's take a bus to the ski area.

02 スキーは初めてですか？

Is it your first time skiing?

03 半日の初心者用スキーレッスンを申し込みましょう。

You might want to take a half-day lesson for beginners.

04 スキーウエアと道具はスキー場で借ります。

We'll rent ski wear and ski gear at the ski resort.

05 スキー靴のサイズはピッタリ合いますか？ 合わなかったら足が痛くなりますよ。

Do your ski boots fit you well? If not, they may hurt your feet.

06 ニセコでは英語でスキーレッスンが受けられます。

You can take a ski lesson in English in Niseko.

07 ケガをしないように気を付けてくださいね。

Be careful not to get injured.

08 スキーの後は温泉に行きましょう。

Let's take a bath at a hot spring after skiing.

09 カフェテリアでランチにしましょう。ここはセルフサービスです。

Let's have lunch in the cafeteria. This is a self-service restaurant.

10 ここのブタ丼がおいしいですよ。券売機で食券を買いましょう。

The pork bowls here are good. Let's buy tickets from the vending machine.

55語ガイド

ニセコへスキーに行きましょう！　バス代とスキーリフト券のセット券を買いましょう。スキーは初めてですか？　私は学校の体育で習いました。しばらく滑っていませんが、今日は私も滑ります。道具は借りましょう。最初はレッスンを受けた方がいいです。ケガをしない転び方を教えてもらえますよ。

体験／スキー場

Let's go skiing in Niseko! We'll buy a set ticket that includes both the bus and the ski lift. Will it be your first time to ski? I learned skiing in PE classes in school. It's been a long time since I last skied. We'll rent ski gear. You should take a ski lesson for beginners. They will teach you how to fall the right way so that you don't injure yourself.

ナルホドAtoZ

R　会社の招待旅行のマレーシア人。
初日に一人の女性が生理になった。
同僚男性たちが薬局に走る。なんてオープンなんだ！

Part2 / Enjoy Hokkaido Life!

34 スノーモービル / Snowmobiles

新雪の上を走ります！
They run on fresh snow!

01 スノーモービル体験をしましょう。

Let's take a snowmobile program.

02 長靴やスキーウエアは無料で貸してくれます。

Boots and ski wear are provided free of charge.

03 まずは保険に入ります。この用紙に名前と生年月日を記入してください。

First, we have to buy insurance. Fill in your name and your birthdate on this form.

04 長靴をはき、スキーウエアを着て、手袋をし、ヘルメットをかぶります。

Put on the boots, ski wear, gloves and helmet.

05 エンジンスイッチには触らないでください。インストラクターが操作します。

Do not touch the engine switch. Your instructor will turn it on for you.

06 スノーモービルの操作はすべて手で行います。

You only use your hands to operate a snowmobile.

07 右手の握りの部分を内側に回すとスピードが出ます。

To accelerate, turn the right hand grip toward you.

08 左手のレバーはブレーキです。自転車と同じように握ってブレーキをかけます。

The lever on the left side is the brake. Just squeeze it like the brake on a bicycle.

09 ハンドルは自分が進みたい方に向けます。

Turn the handlebar to the direction you want to go.

10 インストラクターが手を上げたら「止まれ」のサインですよ。

When your instructor raises his hand, it means stop.

55語ガイド

北海道各地でスノーモービル体験ができます。やってみたいですか？ 会場に着いたら最初に、平地で10分間ほど操作法の指導を受けます。それから、インストラクターの先導で林や山の中につくられたコースを走ります。楽しいですよ！

You can experience snowmobiling at many places in Hokkaido. Do you want to try? OK. When we arrive at the snowmobile site, we'll spend ten minutes beforehand learning how to operate the vehicle. Then you just follow your instructor along the course through the forest or over the hills. It's great fun!

Hokkaido

17 北海道銘菓「わかさいも」には海藻が入っている。さて何だ？
① ワカメ　② ヒジキ　③ コンブ

答え：③　大福豆の餡にコンブ、サツマイモの繊維を混ぜてある。

Part2／Enjoy Hokkaido Life!

35 ワカサギ釣り / Smelt Fishing

テントの中に入って釣りましょう！
Let's fish inside a tent!

01 ワカサギは体長10センチぐらいの小魚です。

***Wakasagi* smelt is a small fish only 10 centimeters in length.**

02 湖や川に厚い氷が張ると氷上ワカサギ釣りができます。

When the ice covering a lake or river is thick enough, people can go ice-fishing for *wakasagi* smelt.

03 色とりどりのテントが見えるでしょう。今日はあそこで釣ります。

See those tents of various colors over there? That's where we'll fish.

04 まずは、代金を払い、釣りの道具を受け取ってから自分の釣り場所を決めます。

First, we pay the fee and get our fishing gear. Then we'll decide where to fish.

05 ねじ回しのような道具を使い、氷に直径15センチほどの穴をあけます。

Using a special drill, we make a hole 15 cm in diameter through the ice.

06 針にエサをつけて、釣り糸を垂らしましょう。

We put the bait on the hook and cast our fishing line.

07 あっ、竿が動いています。引きあげましょう。2匹も釣れました！

Wow, the fishing rod is shaking. Pull it up! Oh, you have two!

08 ワカサギが氷の上で跳ねています。

The *wakasagi* smelt are jumping on the ice.

55語ガイド

今日はワカサギ釣りに茨戸湖に行きます。家から車で1時間です。厚いダウンジャケットを着て、靴の中には使い捨てカイロを入れましょう。風が冷たいので、テントの中に入って釣った方がいいですね。釣れたワカサギは氷上で天ぷらにして食べます。終わったら近くの温泉で温まって帰りましょう。

体験 ワカサギ釣り

Let's go *wakasagi* smelt fishing on Barato Lake. It is a one-hour drive from my house. You need to wear a thick down jacket and put heat packs in your shoes. The wind is very cold, so we'd better fish from inside the tent. We can cook our fresh catch right there on the ice. And before we go home, let's warm ourselves up with a bath in the nearby hot spring.

ナルホド A to Z

S 「ベストな北海道を3日で回りたい」と米国人夫妻。千歳から真っ直ぐ黒岳登山、続いて知床クルーズ、最後は支笏湖でカヌー。「ホッカイドウ、ワンダフル!!」。目が回らなかった？

アジア編❷ You Know What?

●フィリピン

国土	29万9400㎢(日本の約8割)、7000以上の島からなる
人口	9234万人(2010年現在)
首都	マニラ
民族	マレー系が95%だが、100以上の民族が暮らす
宗教	カトリック83%。イスラム教の地域も
飛行機で	東京から約4時間
日本の100円は?	38フィリピンペソ(2014年現在)
日本が正午なら	午前11時(マイナス1時間)
こんにちは	マガンダン　ハポン
ありがとう	サラマット
Masako's view	熱心なカトリック信者が多く、日曜日には教会へ行きたがる。大らかで明るいのはいいけれど、冬の北海道にビーチサンダル履きで来るのはどう?

●マレーシア

国土	33万㎢(日本の約90%)
人口	2995万人(2013年現在)
首都	クアラルンプール
民族	マレー系67%、中国系25%、インド系7%など
宗教	国教はイスラム教。他に仏教、ヒンズー教など
飛行機で	東京から約6時間半
日本の100円は?	2.8マレーシアリンギット(2014年現在)
日本が正午なら	午前11時(マイナス1時間)
こんにちは	スラマット　プタン
ありがとう	トゥリマ　カシ
Masako's view	イスラム系は礼拝を欠かさない人が多く、お祈りのじゅうたんを持って旅行するグループも。女性が持つスカーフの数は「数えきれないほどたくさん」だとか。

●香港

国土	1103㎢(札幌市より少し小さい)
人口	717万人(2013年現在。北海道の1.6倍)
首都	(中華人民共和国の特別行政区)
民族	約95%が漢民族。その他、多民族からなる
宗教	仏教、道教など
飛行機で	東京から約4、5時間
日本の100円は?	6.6ホンコンドル(2014年現在)
日本が正午なら	午前11時(マイナス1時間)
こんにちは	ネイ　ホウマー
ありがとう	トウチェ　ネイ
Masako's view	自分の意見をはっきり言う人が多い。長時間歩くのが嫌いで、「運河沿いを歩きましょうか?」と聞いたら、「なぜ歩くの?」と言われたことも。

＊各データは外務省HPなどを参照しました

Part 3

Discover Hokkaido!
[ザ・北海道]

アジア人に人気の ザ・北海道ベスト10
①真っ白な雪 ②刺し身や魚 ③トウキビとジャガイモ ④アイスクリーム ⑤ラベンダーと花畑
⑥紅葉と落ち葉 ⑦親切で安心な人々 ⑧温泉 ⑨時間に正確な乗り物 ⑩清潔な街の中

Part3 / Discover Hokkaido!

36 クラーク博士 / Dr. Clark | ボーイズ・ビー・アンビシャス！ "Boys, be ambitious!"

CD-36

01 明治政府は多くの外国人を雇うことで日本の近代化を図りました。

To modernize Japan, the Meiji government employed many foreigners.

02 北海道開拓使には約80人の外国人が雇われました。

About 80 foreigners were hired by the Hokkaido Colonization Commission.

03 彼らは教育、鉱山、鉄道、農業などの分野で貢献しました。

They worked in various fields such as education, mining, railway construction and farming.

04 1875年に札幌農学校が創設されました。現在の北海道大学です。

In 1875, Sapporo Agricultural College, present-day Hokkaido University, was built.

05 札幌農学校には約20人が1期生として入学しました。

In the first year, about 20 students enrolled in Sapporo Agricultural College.

06 札幌農学校では生物や化学などの授業が英語で行われました。

At Sapporo Agricultural College, some subjects such as biology and chemistry were taught in English.

07 1876年にアメリカ人のクラーク博士が札幌農学校の教頭になりました。

In 1876, Dr. Clark, an American, became the vice president of Sapporo Agricultural College.

08 クラーク博士は熱心な教育者で、多くの学生に慕われました。

Dr. Clark was a dedicated and enthusiastic educator, and many students admired him.

09 クラーク博士の別れの言葉"ボーイズ・ビー・アンビシャス！"（「少年よ、大志を抱け」）は学生たちを感動させました。

Dr. Clark inspired his students with his parting words "Boys, be ambitious!".

55語ガイド

羊ケ丘展望台からは札幌の街並みが見えます。銀色に輝く正面の建物は野球やサッカーの試合が行われる札幌ドームで、右手を高く挙げている像はクラーク博士です。"真理"のある方向を示しているそうです。私たちも彼の像の前に行き、同じポーズで写真を撮りませんか。

From Hitsujigaoka Observation Hill, we can see the city of Sapporo. The silver building in the foreground is Sapporo Dome, a stadium for baseball and soccer. Look at the statue with the right arm raised high. It is Dr. Clark. They say, "His fingers are pointing to the place where the truth can be found". Shall we pose like this for a photo in front of his statue?

クイズ Hokkaido

18 かつて登別温泉では、やって来るお客さんが多いかどうかを建物の中のある変化で知った。それは何？
①電球の明るさ　②水道の勢い　③畳の湿気

答え：①　温泉街の電気と電車会社に発電所から供給されていたが、電車が走ると電気が足りず電球が暗くなった。

Part3 ／ Discover Hokkaido!

37 三松正夫と有珠山
Mr. Masao Mimatsu and Mt. Usu

CD-37

昭和新山の麓に三松さんの像が建っています。
A statue of Mr. Mimatsu stands at the foot of Mt. Showa-shinzan.

01 有珠山は20世紀に4回爆発しています。
Mt. Usu erupted 4 times in the 20th century.

02 三松さんは1910年の有珠山噴火の時から、火山に強い興味を抱くようになりました。
When he saw the eruption of Mt. Usu in 1910, Mr. Mimatsu became interested in volcanoes.

03 1943年に有珠山が噴火した時、三松さんは地元の郵便局長でした。
When Mt. Usu erupted again in 1943, he was a local postmaster.

04 戦争中だったため、噴火は戦況への悪い予兆として公表されませんでした。
The eruption was kept secret because Japan was at war, and the eruption was regarded as a bad omen.

05 三松さんは昭和新山が形成される様子を記録しました。
Mr. Mimatsu recorded the formation of Mt. Showa-shinzan.

06 1945年に407メートルの昭和新山が誕生しました。
By 1945, the 407-meter-high Mt. Showa-shinzan was formed.

07 硫黄採掘によって山が荒らされないように、三松さんは山を買いました。
To protect it from sulfur mining, Mr. Mimatsu bought Mt. Showa-shinzan.

08 三松さんは89年の生涯に3回、有珠山の噴火を目撃しました。
He died at the age of 89. During his lifetime, he witnessed three eruptions of Mt. Usu.

09 現在、昭和新山は三松さんの家族が所有しています。

Even now, Mt. Showa-shinzan is still owned by the Mimatsu family.

有珠山など北海道内の活発な5つの活火山は、24時間体制で観測が続けられています。2000年3月に有珠山の噴火が迫っていることが予測されました。緊急の避難勧告が出され、1万人の周辺住民全員がわずか3日間で避難し、その直後に噴火が起きました。そのため、一人の犠牲者も出ませんでした。

ザ・北海道　三松正夫と有珠山

In Hokkaido, five very active volcanoes are monitored round the clock. Thanks to this monitoring, an imminent eruption of Mt. Usu was predicted in March in 2000. An emergency evacuation order was issued and all 10,000 local residents were successfully evacuated in just three days! Thanks to this, the eruption caused no casualties.

ナルホドA to Z

T 「便秘なのでカンチョウが欲しい」と言うアジア人。買った薬を薬局のトイレで挿すことになったが、20分たっても出てこない。「大丈夫?」「5本差したけどまだ効かない」。ひえー。その日の午後はトイレ探しに忙しかった。

Part3 / Discover Hokkaido!

38 竹鶴とリタ / Taketsuru and Rita

リタは日本料理が得意でした。
Rita was good at cooking Japanese dishes.

01 竹鶴政孝はウイスキーづくりを学ぶためにスコットランドに来ていました。

Masataka Taketsuru went to Scotland to learn how to distil whiskey.

02 リタはスコットランドの医者の家に生まれました。

Rita was born the daughter of a doctor in Scotland.

03 竹鶴がリタの弟に柔道を教えるためにリタの家を訪れた時、二人は出会いました。

Taketsuru met Rita when he visited her family's house to teach her brother judo.

04 二人は恋に落ちましたが、両家は二人の結婚に反対でした。

They fell in love, but both families objected to their marriage.

05 家族の反対に屈せず、二人はスコットランドで結婚しました。

Undeterred by this opposition, they got married in Scotland.

06 日本で本物のウイスキーをつくりたいという竹鶴の夢にリタは協力しようと思いました。

Rita decided to help Taketsuru to realize his dream of making genuine whiskey in Japan.

07 竹鶴のスコットランドでの研修が終わると、竹鶴はリタと日本にやってきました。

When Taketsuru finished his training in Scotland, he took her with him back to Japan.

08 竹鶴はサントリーに入社し、日本初のウイスキー蒸留所を京都につくりました。

Employed by Suntory, Taketsuru built Japan's first whiskey distillery in Kyoto.

09 1934年に竹鶴は独立して、スコットランドと似た気候の余市にニッカウヰスキー工場を建てました。

In 1934, Taketsuru left Suntory and built his own whiskey distillery in Yoichi. He thought the climate of Yoichi was similar to that of Scotland.

10 リタは生涯竹鶴を支え、彼の夢を一緒に生きたのです。

Rita supported Taketsuru and shared his dream.

ザ・北海道 竹鶴とリタ

リタの日本での暮らしは楽しいことばかりではありませんでした。第2次世界大戦中、対戦国である英国出身のリタは大変つらい思いをしました。スパイ活動を警戒されたこともありました。リタは一生日本で暮らし、余市で亡くなりました。リタの波乱の生涯はテレビドラマになりました。

Life in Japan was not always kind to Rita. During the Second World War, she was suspected of being a spy because she was from Scotland. Rita never returned to her homeland, living her whole life in Japan and dying in Yoichi. Her eventful life was made into a popular TV drama.

クイズ Hokkaido

19 ヒグマの出産はいつ？
① 目覚めたばかりの春　② 木の実で満腹になった秋
③ 冬眠している冬

答え：③　ヒグマはふつう「2月1日生まれ」で年齢を計算する。

Part3 / Discover Hokkaido!

39 マリモ / *Marimo*

マリモはなぜ丸いの？
Why do *marimo* grow in the shape of a ball?

CD-39

01 マリモは緑色の糸状の藻が集まって丸くなったものです。

A *marimo*, or moss ball, consists of green algae filaments.

02 マリモは日本では阿寒湖にだけ生育します。

In Japan, *marimo* grow only in Lake Akan.

03 マリモはベルベットのような柔らかな手触りです。

***Marimo* have a soft velvety texture.**

04 マリモは直径30センチにまで成長しますが、大きくなると崩れて、糸状の藻に戻ります。

A *marimo* can grow up to 30 cm in diameter. When it grows too large, it breaks up into algae filaments.

05 遊覧船でマリモセンターへ行き、マリモを見ましょう。

Let's take a pleasure boat to Marimo Center to see *marimo*.

06 瓶に入ったこのマリモは、近くの湖の藻で人工的につくったものです。

This *marimo* in a bottle was artificially made from algae from the nearby lake.

07 マリモは食べられませんよ。でもマリモにそっくりなお菓子やアイスがあります。食べてみますか？

***Marimo* are not edible. But there are sweets and ice cream that look like marimo. Would you like to try some?**

ある新聞記者がマリモにまつわる物語をつくりました。若いアイヌの恋人たちは深く愛し合っていたものの、仲を引き裂かれ、阿寒湖に身投げしました。そのアイヌの恋人たちの魂はマリモとなって永遠に湖に生きるというのです。一方、アイヌ伝説では、阿寒湖にはたくさんのヒシの実があり、それを嫌う神さまがヒシを追い出しました。怒ったヒシの実は湖畔の草を丸めてそれに「湖を汚す」呪いをかけました。それがマリモの起源だというのです。

A newspaper reporter created a *marimo* story. It goes that there was a young Ainu couple deeply in love. But when they were forced to break up, they chose to drown themselves in Lake Akan. Their spirits turned into *marimo* and lived forever in the lake. The Ainu have another story. There were once many *hishi* nuts growing in Lake Akan. The god of the lake didn't like them and expelled them from Lake Akan. The *hishi* nuts got angry, picked some grass from the shore and turned it into a ball. Then they cursed the ball to make the lake water dirty. This cursed grass ball was the first *marimo*.

ナルホドA to Z

U 神社に行くときは「お参りしますか?」と聞いてみよう。かなりの人が「イエス」。車のおはらいや七五三、結婚式などのしきたりを説明してから行こう。

Part3 / Discover Hokkaido!

40 流氷 / Drift Ice

流氷観光船に乗りましょう。
Let's ride an ice breaker.

01 オホーツク海は北半球で流氷が見られる最南の海です。

The Okhotsk Sea is the southernmost sea in the northern hemisphere where drift ice is seen.

02 流氷が接岸する網走市は北緯44度で、イタリアのミラノと同じくらいです。

The city of Abashiri, where drift ice can be seen, is located at 44 degrees north latitude, about the same as Milan, Italy, for example.

03 1月から3月には紋別、網走から流氷観光船が出ます。

Between January and March, ice breakers are operated out of the ports of Monbetsu and Abashiri.

04 流氷観光船は氷を破壊して進みます。氷が割れる時の音は迫力があります。

Ice breakers move steadily forward, breaking the ice as they go. You can hear the dynamic sounds of the ice cracking.

05 流氷ノロッコ号列車に乗ると、車窓からオホーツク沿岸の流氷を眺められます。

Norokko Trains run along the Okhotsk Sea. A ride gives you the chance to see the drift ice from your window.

06 流氷に付いてくるプランクトンを食べにたくさん魚が集まってきます。

A large number of fish come to this area to eat the plankton brought in by the drift ice.

07 流氷麦酒や流氷アイスは流氷をイメージしたきれいな青色をしています。

Drift ice beer and drift ice ice-cream come in beautiful blue colors.

08 流氷の上ではウオーキング、流氷の下ではダイビングが出来ますよ。

We can enjoy walking on the drift ice and even diving under it.

09 流氷の上にはアザラシ、オオワシ、オジロワシの姿が見られます。

Seals, Steller's sea eagles, and white-tailed eagles can be seen on the drift ice.

10 この地域ではクリオネをペットとして冷蔵庫で飼う人がいますよ。

Some people in this area keep sea angels as pets in the fridge.

オホーツクの春は「海明け」で始まります。冬の間、流氷で閉ざされていた港から氷が消えて、やっと漁船が出港できるようになります。春には毛ガニやキンキ、ニシンなどがたくさん獲れます。特にこの時期の毛ガニはおいしいですよ。

For the fishermen along the Ohkotsk Sea, the spring starts with the so-called "opening of the sea". The drift ice in the ports finally melts away, and they can begin fishing. In spring, they haul in big catches of hairy crabs, channel rockfish and herring. Hairy crab is especially tasty this time of year!

 Hokkaido

20 日本で初めての米国人英語教師マクドナルドが最初に訪れたのは焼尻島。次はどの島？
①奥尻島 ②天売島 ③利尻島

答え：③　そして、利尻島から宗谷岬へ渡る。

Part3 / Discover Hokkaido!

タンチョウ / *Tancho*

求愛のダンスを踊っていますよ。

They are performing a courting dance.

01 タンチョウは体長が約1.4メートルで、羽を広げると2メートル以上あります。

Tancho are about 1.4 meters tall. Their large wingspan measures over 2 meters.

02 タンチョウは頭のてっぺんが赤く、羽根は純白で、嘴と羽根先は黒です。

Tancho have a red spot on their crown. They have snow-white feathers and black beaks and wing tips.

03 タンチョウはもともと渡り鳥でしたが、今は釧路湿原に一年中生息しています。

Formerly migratory birds, they now stay in Kushiro Marshland all year round.

04 一度は絶滅したといわれましたが、現在は約1500羽います。

They were once thought to have gone extinct. But there are now about 1,500 of them.

05 冬が求愛の季節で、3月から5月の間に1、2個の卵を産みます。

Winter is the mating season. The females lay one or two eggs between March and May.

06 両親が交代で卵を温め、卵は約1カ月で孵化します。

Parents take turns sitting on the eggs, which hatch in about one month.

07 タンチョウのヒナが親鳥と同じ大きさになって飛べるようになるまでには半年かかります。かれらは3年で成鳥になります。

It takes half a year for *tancho* chicks to grow to the size of an adult and start to fly. They reach full maturity at three years of age.

08 冬になると、タンチョウはエサを求めて湿原から人里に姿を現します。

In winter, *tancho* are easier to see as they come out of the marsh to look for food near villages.

55語ガイド

「鶴は千年生きる」と言われますが、もちろん実際にはそんなに長生きはしません。寿命はだいたい30〜40年です。また、一度パートナーを決めると一生一緒に過ごすと言われます。だから長寿と夫婦円満の象徴です。昔話や折り紙で日本人にはなじみ深い鳥です。

Cranes are said to live one thousand years. Though they don't actually live that long, of course, they do live up to 30 or 40 years, a long life for a bird. So they have to symbolize longevity. Cranes are also a symbol of happy marriage. Once they find their mate, the couple will stay together for life. Cranes are familiar to Japanese people, appearing in folk tales and in *origami*.

ナルホド A to Z

V 神社の手水舎で、本殿に参拝する前のお浄めの手順の説明をする。「最後にひしゃくの柄を洗うのは次に使う人のため」と言うと感動する外国人が多い。

Part3 / Discover Hokkaido!

42 エゾシカ / Ezo Deer

林の中にシカの家族がいます。
You can see a deer family in the forest.

01 エゾシカは日本最大のシカで、北海道にだけ生息します。

The Ezo deer is the largest deer in Japan. They live only in Hokkaido.

02 昔、大雪の冬にエゾシカが多数餓死し、絶滅しかけたことがありました。

In the past, a winter with heavy snowfall caused many deer to starve and brought them close to extinction.

03 一時は保護のためにエゾシカ猟が禁止されました。

At one time, deer hunting was prohibited to protect them.

04 現在、北海道にはエゾシカが60万頭以上いて、その数は年々増加しています。

Now, however, there are over 600,000 deer in Hokkaido and the number is growing.

05 エゾシカは農業や林業に大きな被害を与えています。

Deer cause a great deal of damage to agriculture and forestry.

06 エゾシカと自動車の交通事故は年間約2千件、列車事故は約3千件起きています。

Each year there are some 2,000 traffic accidents involving cars and deer and 3,000 involving trains and deer.

07 最近、エゾシカの数を減らすために、狩猟とシカ肉の食用化が奨励されています。

Currently, to decrease their numbers, hunting deer and eating their meat is encouraged.

08 シカ肉は高タンパク、低脂肪で鉄分が多い栄養食品です。

Venison is nutritious, low in fat, and high in protein and iron.

09 シカ肉バーガー、シカ肉BBQ、シカ肉丼などが北海道各地で食べられますよ。

In Hokkaido, you can enjoy venison in hamburgers, barbecued or even on rice bowls.

オスジカの角は立派ですね。でも、毎年あの角は春に抜け落ち、生えかわるのを知っていましたか？ 角の枝分かれ数でエゾシカの年齢がわかりますよ。3歳なら3枝、4歳で4枝、5歳以上の鹿の角は5枝。あの林の中のシカは何歳でしょうね？

The antlers of the stags look magnificent! But did you know that they fall off every spring and grow back? You can tell the age of the deer by the number of branches on his antlers. A 3-year-old has 3, a 4-year-old 4, and those 5 and older 5 branches. What do you think is the age of that deer you saw in the forest?

クイズ Hokkaido

21 モエレ沼公園の「ガラスのピラミッド」。冷房には何を使う？
① ガス　② 電気　③ 雪

答え：③　約1000トンの雪を冷房として使う。

Part3 ／ Discover Hokkaido!

43 利尻と礼文 / Rishiri and Rebun
利尻島の名物はコンブとウニです。
Rishiri Island is famous for kelp and sea urchin.

01 利尻島と礼文島は日本最北の島です。

Rishiri and Rebun are the northernmost islands in Japan.

02 緯度が高いので、島のあちこちで高山植物が見られます。

As these islands are located at such high latitude, alpine flowers can be seen everywhere.

03 島にはクマとヘビがいないので安心してハイキングを楽しめます。

There are no bears or snakes, so we can enjoy hiking in the mountains without worrying about them.

04 利尻島と礼文島はコンブとウニで有名です。

Both islands are well known for their good kelp and sea urchin.

05 島ではウニとり体験やウニの殻むき体験ができますよ！

Sea urchin gathering and sea urchin shelling programs are offered on the islands.

06 利尻島は、高さ1720メートルの利尻山が噴火して出来た円形の島です。

Rishiri Island is a round island created by the eruption of 1,720-meter high Mt. Rishiri.

07 利尻島の周囲は60キロで、車なら約1時間で1周できます。

The circumference of Rishiri Island is 60 kilometers. It takes one hour to go around it by car.

08 礼文島は細長い平らな島で、高山植物を楽しめる散策路がたくさんあります。

Rebun Island is a long and narrow island with no high mountains. There are many nature trails to enjoy the alpine flowers.

70語ガイド

この石碑の人物は利尻島で一番有名なアメリカ人、ラナルド・マクドナルドさんです。1848年、日本がまだ鎖国中だったとき、マクドナルドは利尻島にやってきました。インディアンの血を引く彼は日本人に憧れたのだそうです。その後、密入国罪で長崎に送られ入獄したのですが、帰国まで彼は日本人に英語を教えました。彼が日本初のネイティブ英語教師です。

Look at this stone monument! It is dedicated to Ranald McDonald, the most famous American on Rishiri Island. In 1848, when Japan was still closed to the outside world, he came to Rishiri Island. As he was half native American, he wanted to meet Japanese. He was caught and sent to prison in Nagasaki. There he taught English to Japanese. He is said to be the first native English teacher in Japan.

ナルホドA to Z

W	アイヌ文様は魔よけの意味もある。切り絵でプレゼントすると喜ばれる。

Part3 / Discover Hokkaido!

摩周湖
Lake Mashu

霧につつまれた神秘の湖です。
A mysterious lake covered with mist

01 摩周湖は周囲が20キロ、水深220メートルの火口湖です。

Lake Mashu is a crater lake with a circumference of 20 kilometers and a depth of 220 meters at its deepest point.

02 摩周湖は透明度がバイカル湖に次ぎ世界第2位です。

It has the second most transparent water in the world, after Lake Baikal.

03 湖の周囲は高く切り立った断崖です。

High steep cliffs surround the lake.

04 湖底からの湧水が対流するので冬の間も凍りません。

Spring water constantly circulating up from the lake bed keeps it from freezing in winter.

05 霧につつまれていることが多いので、「霧の摩周湖」と呼ばれます。

It is called misty Lake Mashu because it is often covered with a thick blanket of fog.

06 摩周ブルー、霧、樹氷というソフトクリームがあります。

They sell soft ice cream by the names of Mashu Blue, Mashu Mist and Silver Frost.

07 摩周湖が霧で覆われていないと、そのカップルは長続きしないと言われますが…。

People say if a couple gets a clear view of the lake, it means they will break up. But I don't think it's true.

摩周湖にある島にはアイヌ伝説があります。アイヌのお婆さんがはぐれた孫を待ちくたびれて島になってしまいました。そのおばあさんの涙がたまって摩周湖が出来ました。人が近付くとお婆さんは孫が来たと思い、喜びの涙を流します。その涙が摩周湖の霧だというのです。今日も摩周湖は深い霧ですね。お婆さんが喜んでいるのかもしれません。

ザ・北海道　摩周湖

There is an Ainu legend about the small island in Lake Mashu. A long time ago, a grandmother was looking for her missing grandchild. After waiting and waiting in vain, she eventually turned into the island. Her tears filled the crater and created Lake Mashu. Whenever she sees a person, she thinks she can finally meet her grandchild and sheds tears of happiness. Today, the lake is thickly covered with mist, so I think the grandmother must be very happy.

クイズ Hokkaido

22 札幌市のひと冬の除雪予算はおよそいくら？
①13億円　②130億円　③1300億円

答え：②　雪対策事業を加えると、除雪関係予算は約180億円！

Part3 / Discover Hokkaido!

45 小樽運河 / Otaru Canal

小樽運河に沿って遊歩道があります。
There is a promenade along Otaru Canal.

01 小樽運河は1923年に完成しました。

Otaru Canal was built in 1923.

02 荷物は港で船から艀(はしけ)に積み替え、運河を通って倉庫に運ばれました。

It carried cargo on barges from ships in port to the warehouses of the city.

03 やがて埠頭が出来て、倉庫に直接荷物が運ばれるようになりました。

A few years later, a large pier was built, enabling the cargo to be carried directly to the warehouses.

04 使われなくなった小樽運河には、泥がたまり悪臭がしました。

Left unused, the water of Otaru Canal became muddy and foul-smelling.

05 運河を完全に埋め立てて道路をつくることが決まりました。

It was decided to fill in the entire canal and construct a road in its place.

06 埋め立てが始まりましたが、運河の保存運動が起こり、工事は中断しました。

Filling-in work was started, but a campaign to preserve the canal succeeded in putting a halt to the project.

07 保存運動派による集会やコンサートには全国から人が集まりました。

The meetings and concerts organized by the preservation group attracted people from around Japan.

08 運河保存運動で小樽運河は全国に知られるようになりました。

The preservation campaign made Otaru Canal famous nationwide.

09 1986年には運河が保存されることになり、運河に沿って遊歩道がつくられ、ガス灯が設置されました。

In 1986, it was officially decided to preserve the canal. A promenade was built along the canal, and gas lamps installed.

10 運河周辺の石造り倉庫はレストランやみやげ店になりました。

Many of the stone warehouses near the canal were turned into restaurants or gift shops.

ザ・北海道 小樽運河

70語ガイド

小樽の観光名所は何といっても運河と古い街並みですね。小樽は20世紀の初めにはニシン漁、石炭出荷、樺太開発などで栄えました。石造りの倉庫や銀行、繊維会社、海運会社の建物がたくさん建てられました。今、その頃の建物は、レストランやホテル、みやげ店になっています。

The canal and the nearby streets with old buildings are the most popular tourist spots in Otaru. In the early 20th century, the port of Otaru served as a base for herring fishing, coal transport, and the development of Sakhalin. Many stone warehouses and banks were built, along with the offices of textile and shipping companies. Now these buildings are used as restaurants, hotels or shops.

ナルホドA to Z

X どこでも見かけるフクロウのおみやげに「なぜ？」。
知恵の神様で、日本語で「ふ（No）苦労（hardship）」だからと説明すると納得する。

Part3／Discover Hokkaido!

46 札幌オリンピック / Sapporo Olympics

CD-46

オリンピックで使われたスキージャンプ場が見えます。

We can see the old Olympic ski jump hill.

01 1972年2月にアジア初の冬季オリンピックが札幌で開かれました。

In February 1972, Sapporo hosted Asia's first ever Winter Olympics.

02 その前年には、冬季オリンピックにやって来る選手や観客のために、札幌で初めての地下鉄が開業しました。

The year before, the city's first subway line began operation in preparation for the arrival of the athletes and spectators.

03 札幌冬季オリンピックには35カ国から約1100人の選手が参加しました。

About 1,100 athletes from 35 countries participated.

04 大倉山の「札幌ウィンタースポーツミュージアム」ではスケートやスキージャンプを疑似体験できます。

At the Winter Sports Museum on Okurayama Hill, simulators offer a chance to experience ski jumping and skating.

05 札幌市は同じ年にオリンピックを開催したミュンヘン市と姉妹都市です。

Sapporo and Munich are sister cities because both hosted the Olympics in the same year.

06 札幌には、オリンピックで使われたスケート、スキー、リュージュの施設があり、今でも使われています。

In Sapporo, the Olympic venues for skating, skiing and luge sledding are still in use.

55語ガイド

札幌の人口は約190万人で、面積は香港と同じぐらいです。冬は寒く雪がたくさん降りますが、暮らしやすい都市ですよ。雑誌の読者調査で、日本で一番好きな都市に何度も選ばれています。都心から車ならわずか30分でスキー場、ゴルフ場、温泉、海水浴場に行けます。

ザ・北海道　札幌オリンピック

The population of Sapporo is about 1.9 million. The city's area is roughly that of Hong Kong's. In winter it is cold and snows a lot. But it is a convenient city to live in. In a magazine survey, Sapporo has been chosen as the favorite city to visit in Japan. Ski runs, golf courses, hot spring resorts and beaches are all within a 30-minute drive from downtown.

クイズ Hokkaido

23 国道12号の日本一長い直線区間は約何キロ？
①29キロ　②39キロ　③49キロ

答え：① 美唄市と滝川市の間にある。

Part3 / Discover Hokkaido!

47 青函トンネル / Seikan Tunnel

青函トンネルは北海道と本州を結んでいます。
Seikan Tunnel connects the islands of Hokkaido and Honshu.

01 青函トンネルは長さ53.9キロで世界最長の海底トンネルです。

Seikan Tunnel is the world's longest undersea tunnel, with the length of 53.9 km.

02 青函トンネルは海底から100メートルの地中につくられています。

The tunnel is constructed 100 meters below the seafloor.

03 海面からは一番深いところで240メートルもあります。

The deepest point is 240 meters below the surface of the sea.

04 青森・函館間は、青函トンネルが出来るまでは連絡船で約4時間かかりました。今では列車で約2時間です。

Before Seikan Tunnel was built, it took 4 hours between Hakodake and Aomori by ferry. Now it is only 2 hours by train.

05 1954年の台風で青函連絡船が沈没したのをきっかけに、トンネルが建設されました。

Construction of the Seikan Tunnel was triggered by the sinking of a Seikan ferry in a typhoon in 1954.

06 2016年に函館まで新幹線が延伸される予定です。

By 2016, the Shinkansen bullet train line is scheduled to be extended to Hakodate.

07 2030年までには札幌と東京が約5時間で結ばれる計画です。

And by 2030, it will connect Tokyo and Sapporo in just 5 hours.

55語ガイド

北海道と本州をトンネルで結ぼうというのは第2次世界大戦前からの夢でした。でも、資金もかかり技術も困難でなかなか実現しませんでした。ところが1954年、台風で青函連絡船が沈没し、千百人以上が亡くなる事故が起きたのです。この事故で計画が一気に具体化し、1988年に世界一長い海底トンネルが完成したのです。

ザ・北海道　青函トンネル

Even before World War II, people dreamed of connecting Hokkaido with Honshu. But the dream was never realized because it was just too expensive and difficult. In 1954, a ferry sank in a typhoon and over 1,100 people were killed. After this tragedy, it was decided to construct the tunnel. Finally in 1988 the world's longest undersea tunnel was completed.

| Y | 梅干し、黒砂糖、抹茶などの飴は日本ならではの味。安くて喜ばれる。 |

Part3 / Discover Hokkaido!

48 ワインとチーズ / Wine and Cheese
CD-48

今日はワイナリー巡りをしましょう。
Let's visit some wineries today.

01 北海道はナチュラルチーズと醸造用ブドウでは日本一の生産量です。

Hokkaido produces the largest amount of natural cheese and wine grapes in Japan.

02 日本初のナチュラルチーズは函館近郊のトラピスト修道院でつくられました。

Japan's first natural cheese was made at a Trappist Monastery on the outskirts of Hakodate.

03 北海道には100以上のチーズ工場があり、見学できるところもあります。

In Hokkaido, there are over 100 cheese factories, and some of them are open to visitors.

04 みそ、笹、桜などの和風チーズがつくられています。

Special Japanese-flavor cheeses are made using ingredients such as *miso*, bamboo leaves, and cherry blossoms.

05 北海道には20軒ほどのワイナリーと50以上のワイン用ブドウ畑があります。

There are some 20 wineries and over 50 vineyards.

06 テイスティングが出来るワイナリーがありますよ。

Some offer wine tasting.

07 レストランやカフェが併設されているワイナリーもあります。

Some wineries also have cafes and restaurants.

08 ブドウ畑を見ながら飲むワインは格別！ 地元のワインには地元のチーズが合いますね。

Wine tastes better when you drink it overlooking the vineyard. And local cheeses go especially well with local wines.

09 北海道のワインづくりの歴史は実は長いのです。

Wine making in Hokkaido actually has quite a long history.

10 1876年に野生の山ブドウを原料に北海道初のワインがつくられました。

The first wine in Hokkaido was made from wild grapes in 1876.

道東の池田町は十勝ワインで有名です。最初は山ブドウを使ってワインづくりをはじめました。町職員がドイツでワインづくりを学び、ブドウの品種改良をするなど努力の結果、やっと国際的に高く評価されるワインが出来たのです。町民だけが買えるお手頃価格のワインもありますよ。ここでの乾杯はもちろんワインです！

The town of Ikeda in eastern Hokkaido is famous for Tokachi wine. They originally used wild grapes. Then town officials went to Germany to learn wine making and also developed new strains of grapes suitable for wine. Eventually Tokachi wine won worldwide recognition! The town offers a special reasonably priced wine for local residents. Of course, they do all their toasting with wine!

クイズ Hokkaido

24 紅葉で有名な北海道で一番高い山は？
①黒岳　②旭岳　③羊蹄山

答え：② 2291メートル

Part3 ／ Discover Hokkaido!

49 サケ / Salmon
サケはなぜ生まれた川が分かるの？
How can a salmon find the river where it was born?

01 北海道では秋になると多くの川でサケが遡上する姿が見られます。

In autumn, salmon are seen swimming upstream in many rivers in Hokkaido.

02 サケは上流で産卵してから死にますが、命は次の世代に引き継がれます。

After spawning in the upper reaches of their home river, the salmon die. Then the salmon life cycle starts all over again.

03 北海道各地のサケの孵化場では、春になると稚魚を放流します。

Hatcheries around Hokkaido release salmon fry in the spring.

04 サケの稚魚は川を下り、北太平洋で生活した後、3〜5年で母川に戻ります。

They swim downstream to the sea, then out to the North Pacific where they grow to maturity, only to return to the river of their birth 3 to 5 years later.

05 何千キロも遠くから母川を探し当てるなんて素晴らしい能力です。

It is amazing they can detect and return to their place of birth from thousands of kilometers away.

06 千歳や札幌にあるサケの科学館に行くと、サケのことが詳しく分かりますよ。

A visit to a salmon museum in Sapporo or Chitose will give you more information on salmon.

70語ガイド

札幌の中心には豊平川が流れています。一時は、この川の水が汚れ、サケが上って来なくなりました。ですが、1970年代に豊平川にサケを呼び戻そうという運動が始まり、川の水をきれいにして稚魚を放流しました。すると数年後、豊平川にサケが戻ってきたのです。札幌市民は感激しました。今では毎年約2千匹のサケがこの川に帰ってきます。

ザ・北海道　サケ

The Toyohira River runs through the center of Sapporo. At one time the water had become so polluted that salmon were no longer able to come upstream to spawn. In the 1970s, however, local people started a campaign to bring back the salmon. They cleaned up the river and released salmon fry. A few years later, the citizens were excited to see salmon swimming upstream once again. The salmon had come back! Now about 2,000 salmon return annually to the Toyohira River.

ナルホドAtoZ

Z 日本では夏の間中、花火がコンビニやスーパーで手に入るので驚かれる。
アメリカでは独立記念日だけ。

イスラム編 / You Know What?

北海道にはイスラム圏からの旅行者も急増中！ イスラム教徒の習慣にあわせた気遣いを。

●お祈りについて

- 1日5回という人たち（旅行中はホテルの自室と、昼ごはんの後だけでOKな人も多い）、旅行中は自室でのお祈り以外は省略するという人。いろいろなので、どうしたいか聞いたほうが良い。
- メッカの「カーバ神殿」は、北海道からはほぼ西北西の方向（厳密でなくてもOK）。方角はスマホで簡単に調べられる。
- 北海道内のモスク（イスラム教の礼拝堂）や、空港、ショッピングモール、繁華街などでの礼拝スペースを知っておく。

●食べ物

- 豚肉は口にしない。豚骨スープもラードもダメ。
- アルコールは飲まない。食品の加工過程で使われていてもダメ。
- でも、外国旅行中はあまり厳しく守らない人たちもいる。
- おすすめは魚かハラール食品（イスラム向けに処理した食肉など）。
- 札幌市内にはハラールレストランがある。

イスラム教の人への声掛け英語

●食事の時にはこう聞いてみよう。

①どんな食べ物が食べられますか？
What foods can you eat?
②これは食べてもいい食べ物ですか？
Are you allowed to eat this?
③これはハラールの食べ物です。
This dish is halal.
④この料理には豚肉が使われていません。
This dish does not have pork in it.
⑤このラーメンのスープは豚骨からとっています。
This *ramen* dish uses pork bones to make broth.
⑥このそばの出汁は魚と海藻でとりました。
Fish and seaweed are used for the soup of this buckwheat noodle.
⑦このみそにはアルコールが使われています。
This *miso* contains some alcohol.

●お祈りしたいか聞いてみよう。

①今、止まってお祈りしたいですか？
Would you like to stop now to pray?
②今日は何時にお祈りしたいですか？
What times today do you want to pray?
③このショッピングモールにはイスラム教の礼拝所があります。
You can pray in the prayer room at this shopping mall.
④メッカの方角は北海道からは西北西です。こちらですよ。
From Hokkaido, west north west is the direction to Mecca. I think this way.

資料編

知っておきたい！
ガイドの基本ABC

アロマ・コスメが人気

アジア人に人気の 北海道みやげベスト10 <その他編>
①ラベンダーポプリ、まくら ②馬油 ③化粧品 ④顔用パック ⑤100円ショップの商品 ⑥文房具
⑦ハローキティグッズ ⑧北一硝子の醤油差し ⑨ユニクロの服 ⑩イッセイミヤケの服

1. 単位の換算

●重さ（体重や荷物）
※概算で一桁まで四捨五入

キロ kg	ポンド lb
1	2.2

キロ kg	ポンド lb
0.45	1

〈60キロのあなたは何ポンド？〉

kg	45	50	55	60	65	70	75	80
lb	99	110	121	132	143	154	165	176

●高さと長さ　山の高さ
※概算で一桁まで四捨五入

メートル m	フィート ft	ヤード yd	インチ in
1	3.3	1.1	39.4

〈あの山の高さをフィートにすると〉

	藻岩山	駒ケ岳	羊蹄山	旭岳
メートル	531	1,131	1,898	2,291
フィート	1,752	3,732	6,263	7,560

●背の高さ〈センチからフィートへ〉

Cm	150	155	160	165	170	175	180	185
Ft/Inch	4'11"	5'1"	5'3"	5'5"	5'7"	5'9"	5'11"	6'1"

（注）インチは十二進法。4'11"の読み方は4フィート11インチ

●距離
※概算で一桁まで四捨五入

キロメートル km	マイル mile
1	0.6
1.6	1

●速度〈車のスピードは？〉

キロメートル km/h	マイル mile/h
1	0.6
1.6	1

●広さ(大) 〈公園や都市の広さ〉

平方キロメートル(km²)	ヘクタール(ha)	エーカー(ac)
1	100	247.1

※(100a=1ha)／1エーカーは約0.4ヘクタール

●広さ(小) 〈パッチワークの布を買うとき〉

平方メートル	平方フィート	平方ヤード
1	10.8	1.2

●体積 〈ガソリンや水の量〉

リットル	英ガロン	米ガロン
1	0.22	0.26

※ガソリンの値段の比較によく使う

●洋服のサイズ換算

日本	7	9	11	13	15
アメリカ	8	10	12	14	16
イギリス	32	34	36	38	40

資料編

●年号の換算 〈日本の年号は西暦にするのが大変。でもこれさえあれば大丈夫〉

明治：67をプラス　　（例：明治10年　西暦1877年）
大正：11をプラス　　（例：大正5年　西暦1916年）
昭和：25をプラス　　（例：昭和40年　西暦1965年）
平成：12をマイナス　（例：平成2年＝1990年　平成20年＝2008年）

●温度の換算

アメリカ人への温度の説明は大変。華氏を摂氏に、摂氏を華氏に。
温度のアバウト換算、試してみよう。

〈華氏°Fから摂氏°Cへ〉換算表：アメリカの温度から日本の温度に

°F	0	10	20	30	40	50	60	70	80	90	100
°C	−18	−12	−7	−1	4	10	16	21	27	32	38

（注）°Fから°Cへ：正確には　（華氏温度−32）×5÷9

〈摂氏°Cから華氏°Fへ〉換算表：日本の温度からアメリカの温度に

°C	−10	−5	0	5	10	15	20	25	30	35	40
°F	14	23	32	41	50	59	68	77	86	95	104

（注）°Cから°Fへ：正確には　摂氏温度÷5×9+32

2. 日本の祝日と行事

●日本の祝日:National Holidays in Japan(年に15日)

1月1日	元旦	New Year's Day
1月第2月曜日	成人の日	Coming-of-age Day
2月第2月曜日	建国記念の日	National Founding Day
3月21日ごろ	春分の日	Vernal Equinox Day
4月29日	昭和の日	The Day of Showa
5月3日	憲法記念日	Constitution Memorial Day
5月4日	みどりの日	Greenery Day
5月5日	こどもの日	Children's Day/Boy's Festival
7月第3月曜日	海の日	Marine Day
9月第3月曜日	敬老の日	Respect-for-the-Aged Day
9月23日ごろ	秋分の日	Autumnal Equinox Day
10月第2月曜日	体育の日	Sport Day
11月3日	文化の日	Culture Day
11月23日	勤労感謝の日	Labor Thanksgiving Day
12月23日	天皇誕生日	Emperor's Birthday

●年中行事(お盆と七夕は北海道での日にち)

1月1~7日	お正月	New Year's holidays
2月3日	節分豆まき	Bean-throwing Ceremony
2月14日	バレンタインデー	Valentine's Day
3月3日	ひな祭り	Doll's Festival
5月5日	こどもの日	Children's Day
8月7日	七夕	The Star Festival
8月14~16日	お盆	Bon Festival
9月中旬	お月見	Moon Viewing
12月31日	大晦日	New Year's Eve

3. 植物と果物

●サクラ

日本の国花	the national flower of Japan
サクラの木	cherry tree
サクラの花	cherry blossom
花見	cherry blossom viewing
花見の宴	cherry-blossom-viewing party
サクラ前線	cherry blossom front

●北海道の草花

ラベンダー	lavender
ヒマワリ	sun flower
シバザクラ	moss pink
タンポポ	dandelion
チューリップ	tulip
ソバの花	buckwheat flower
フキノトウ	giant butterbur's spring growth
イタドリ	Japanese knotweed
ハマナス	Japanese rose
アジサイ	hydrangea
サビタ	hydrangea paniculata

●北海道で見かける樹木

*針葉樹	conifers
トドマツ	Sakhalin fir
エゾマツ	ezo-spruce
アカエゾマツ	Sakhalin spruce
カラマツ	larch
*広葉樹	broad-leaved trees
シラカバ	Japanese white birch
ブナ	Siebold's beech
ニセアカシア	black locust
イタヤカエデ	painted maple
ナナカマド	mountain ash
イチョウ	gingko
ニレ	elm
スギ	cedar

●北海道の果物

果樹園	orchard
果物狩り	fruit picking
サクランボ	cherry
スイカ	watermelon
メロン	melon
ブルーベリー	blueberry
ナシ	pear
イチゴ	strawberry
プラム	plum
ハスカップ	blue honeysuckle

4. 農水産物と食べ物

●北海道でたくさん収穫される農産物

ビート	beet
ジャガイモ	potato
トウモロコシ	corn
大豆	soy bean
米	rice

●北海道の畑の恵み

ソバ	buckwheat
小豆	azuki bean
アスパラ	asparagus
百合根	lily bulb
ナガイモ	chinese yam

●北海道で水揚げの多い海産物

ホタテ	scallop
サケ	salmon
タラ	cod
ほっけ	Atka mackerel
サンマ	Pacific saury

●説明しにくい食べ物はこう表現

It's a kind of (一種の)	flat fish	カレイ
	river fish	川魚
	sea fish	海の魚
	potato	イモ
	seaweed	海草
	vegetable	野菜

●北海道で人気の魚や貝

カジカ	Japanese sculpin
アンコウ	goosefish
キンキ	channel rockfish
シシャモ	shishamo smelt
ソイ	jacopever
ハタハタ	Japanese sandfish
ハッカク	sailfin poacher
アワビ	abalone
ホッキ	Sakhalin surf clam
ニシン	herring
カスベ	stingray
カキ	oyster
ホヤ	sea squirt

●「寿司食いねぇ」ネタは？

マグロ	tuna
トロ	fatty tuna
ブリ	yellowtail
サケ	salmon
ウニ	sea urchin
イクラ	salmon roe
タコ	octopus
イカ	squid
タイ	sea bream
ホタテ	scallop
エビ	shrimp
シメサバ	marinated mackerel
カズノコ	herring roe

●北海道で人気のある食べ物

ジンギスカン	Genghis khan/Jingisukan
スープカレー	soup curry
ラーメン	ramen
石狩鍋	Ishikari nabe hot-pot
チャンチャン焼き	grilled salmon & vegetables in *miso* sauce
ソフトクリーム	soft ice cream
ワイン	wine

●家庭料理

キンピラ	cooked burdock root and carrot
肉ジャガ	cooked pork and potato
豚汁	pork and vegetable *miso* soup
つけもの	pickled vegetables
茶碗蒸し	egg custard
焼き魚	grilled fish
コロッケ	croquette
カレーライス	curry and rice
お茶漬け	rice in soup
梅干し	pickled plum
納豆	fermented soy beans
おにぎり	rice ball

●甘味処で一休み

懐紙	paper napkin for tea and sweets
お団子	Japanese sweet dumpling
お汁粉	Japanese sticky rice cake in sweet bean soup
ミツマメ	seaweed jelly and beans with sweet syrup
ドラヤキ	Japanese pancake sandwich
カキ氷	shaved ice with syrup
トコロテン	seaweed jelly with salty dressing
塩昆布	salted dried kelp
抹茶	powdered green tea
緑茶	green tea
番茶	roasted green tea

資料編

5. 地理

●火山の3種類

死火山	extinct volcano
休火山	dormant volcano
活火山	active volcano

●火山の英語

噴火	eruption
地震	earthquake
火口	crater
噴煙	spew/smoke
溶岩	lava
土石流	mud (debris) slide
火砕流	pyroclastic flow
警報	warning
避難	evacuation
仮設住宅	temporary housing

●温泉のいろいろ

温度	temperature
露天風呂	open air bath
鉱物	minerals
硫黄	sulfur
湯治	bathing for medicinal purposes
秘湯	hot springs in the remote area
混浴	mixed bath

6. 生き物

●北海道の代表的な動物

エゾオコジョ	Ezo stoat
エゾシカ	Ezo deer
エゾリス	Ezo squirrel
エゾモモンガ	Ezo flying squirrel
キタキツネ	red fox
ゼニガタアザラシ	harbor seal
ナキウサギ	rock rabbit/northern pika
ヒグマ	brown bear

●北海道の代表的な鳥

エトピリカ	tufted puffin
ウミガラス（オロロン鳥）	common guillemot
オオワシ	Steller's sea eagle
オジロワシ	white-tailed sea eagle
シマフクロウ	Blakiston's fish owl
タンチョウ	red-crested crane （Japanese crane）

●旭山動物園の人気者

ゴマフアザラシ	spotted seal
ペンギン	penguin
ホッキョクグマ	polar bear
オランウータン	orangutan
カピバラ	capybara
クモザル	spider monkey

●小樽水族館の生き物たち

ハンマーヘッドシャーク	hammer head shark
クリオネ	sea angel
セイウチ	walrus
オタリア	South American sea lion
アゴヒゲアザラシ	bearded seal
クラゲ	jelly fish

7. スポーツ&レジャー

●北海道のスポーツ

カーリング	curling
スキー	skiing/downhill skiing
歩くスキー	cross country skiing
スケート	ice skating
スノーボード	snowboarding
カヌー	canoeing
乗馬	horse riding
ハンググライダー	hang gliding
熱気球	hot air ballooning
ラフティング	rafting
プロ野球	professional baseball
地元のチーム	local team
好きな選手	favorite player
監督	manager
シャトルバス	shuttle bus
札幌ドーム	Sapporo Dome

●花火大会　Fireworks display

新聞社主催	sponsored by newspaper companies
河畔	river banks
蒸し暑い	muggy
蚊	mosquito
虫よけスプレー	insect repellent spray
蚊さされ	mosquito bite
綿アメ	cotton candy
初恋	first love
浴衣	cotton kimono
下駄	clogs

●流行モノ　fads and fashions

アニメ	anime/comics (Dragonball, Akira etc)
インターネット喫茶	Internet café
マンガ喫茶	comics café
オタク	geek
メイド喫茶	maid café
カプセルホテル	capsule hotel
手相占い	palm reading
スピリチャルカウンセラー	psychic
コスプレ	cosplay
アニメキャラ	animation character
お化け屋敷	spooky house
ご当地キャラ	local mascot

●修学旅行

修学旅行	school trip
班	group
制服	school uniform
ジャージ	sweat suit/pants/shirt
お土産	souvenir
地図	map
街角	street corner
携帯	cell phone
枕投げ	pillow fight

資料編

遠藤昌子
（えんどう・まさこ）

北海道留萌市出身。慶応義塾大学卒業。米オハイオ州ハイデルバーグ大学日本校で教育学修士を取得。英検1級、会議通訳2級、TOEIC990点。2003年に英語通訳案内士免許を取得し、欧米、アジア各国からの訪問者に英語で北海道を紹介するとともに、外国クルーズ船上でのレクチャー、通訳案内士対象のセミナー講師などを務める。趣味は旅行。Sapporo English Guides代表、日本観光通訳協会理事。
著書に『PERAPERAホッカイドー　英語で北海道をガイドする本』（アマンダ・ハーロウとの共著、北海道新聞社）がある。

編集：	仮屋志郎（北海道新聞社）
企画・編集協力：	山口英子
英文校正・ナレーション：	アマンダ・ハーロウ
イラスト：	ヨウコング
ブックデザイン：	佐々木正男（佐々木デザイン事務所）
付録CD制作：	（株）リレック／有限会社フィクス

英語でホッカイドー
PERAPERAトーク500

2015年3月5日　初版第1刷発行

著　者　　遠藤昌子
発行者　　松田敏一
発行所　　北海道新聞社
　　　　　〒060-8711　札幌市中央区大通西3丁目6
　　　　　出版センター（編集）電話011-210-5742
　　　　　　　　　　　（営業）電話011-210-5744
　　　　　http://shop.hokkaido-np.co.jp/book/
印　刷　　札幌大同印刷株式会社

乱丁・落丁本は出版センター（営業）にご連絡くださればお取り換えいたします。
ISBN978-4-89453-771-2
© ENDO Masako, 2015, Printed in Japan
本書および付録CDの無断複製は著作権法上の例外を除き禁じられています。